GERMANY IN THE AGE OF KAISER WILHELM II

Studies in European History

Series Editors: Richard Overy
John Breuilly
Peter Wilson

Published Titles

GERMANY IN THE AGE OF
KAISER WILHELM II

JAMES RETALLACK

First published 1996 by
MACMILLAN PRESS LTD
Houndmills, Basingstoke, Hampshire RG21 6XS
and London
Companies and representatives
throughout the world

A catalogue record for this book is available
from the British Library.

ISBN 0–333–59242–5

 First published in the United States of America 1996 by
ST. MARTIN'S PRESS, INC.
Scholarly and Reference Division,
175 Fifth Avenue,
New York, N.Y. 10010
ISBN 0–312–16031–3

Library of Congress Cataloging-in-Publication Data applied for

10 9 8 7 6 5 4 3
09 08 07 06 05 04 03 02

Printed in Malaysia

This book is for Helen

Contents

List of Figures

A Note on References

References are cited throughout in brackets according to the numbering in the select bibliography, with semi-colons separating each item. Page references, where necessary, are indicated by a colon after the bibliography number.

Editor's Preface

The main purpose of this new series of studies is to make available to teacher and student alike developments in a field of history that has become increasingly specialised with the sheer volume of new research and literature now produced. These studies are designed to present the 'state of the debate' on important themes and episodes in European history since the sixteenth century, presented in a clear and critical way by someone who is closely concerned himself with the debate in question.

The studies are not intended to be read as extended bibliographical essays, though each will contain a detailed guide to further reading which will lead students and the general reader quickly to key publications. Each book carries its own interpretation and conclusions, while locating the discussion firmly in the centre of the current issues as historians see them. It is intended that the series will introduce students to historical approaches which are in some cases very new and which, in the normal course of things, would take many years to filter down into the textbooks and school histories. I hope it will demonstrate some of the excitement historians, like scientists, feel as they work away in the vanguard of their subject.

The format of the series conforms closely with that of the companion volumes of studies in economic and social history which has already established a major reputation since its inception in 1968. Both series have an important contribution to make in publicising what it is that historians are doing and in making history more open and accessible. It is vital for history to communicate if it is to survive.

R. J. OVERY

Preface

'We stand within the continuity and community of historians – our predecessors, our teachers, our colleagues, our students – who have preceded us and taught us, who inspire and provoke us, who critique and revise [our views]. . . . We are dwarfs on the shoulders of giants' [192]. Shortly before his death, Thomas Nipperdey wrote these lines to convey his gratitude to those who had sustained him in the task of writing the most comprehensive account of imperial Germany we have today. Nipperdey's words are especially compelling in an age when scholarship is still afflicted by the publish-or-perish syndrome. How many books today begin by debunking the work of those who first ventured into uncharted territory? How many promise the latest model or interpretation, invariably guaranteed to make previous research obsolete and transform the field forever?

This state of affairs can have two particularly unfortunate consequences. On the one hand it restricts the sense of community among colleagues who must continually strive to break down barriers to fruitful scholarly dialogue. On the other hand it leaves students bewildered. The weaker students express dismay that the 'experts' cannot agree on what actually happened in history. Even the more capable ones ask why historians spend so much time explaining what *didn't* happen, or what *should* have happened. Still others wonder why established scholars so often talk past each other, why academics insist that their critics have not properly 'understood' their latest book, and why the postmodern monograph appears to dismiss history's master narrative as unknowable or *passé*.

This book was written partly to foster better communication among historians, and partly to address these student complaints. Although reading for this project increased my appreciation of the richness and sophistication of previous work on Wilhelmine

Germany, some of that richness is necessarily squeezed out of this short account, in order to bring central themes and problems into sharper focus. I particularly regret that it was not possible to deal more systematically with literature offering a comparative perspective on Wilhelmine Germany. Events since 1989 only underscore the need to consider Germany's place within an evolving Europe. I would also have liked to draw more fully on the documentary sources available. I recognise that some colleagues will question my decisions about when to emphasise traditional or revisionist approaches, when to cite certain works and not others, and when to treat one topic more fully than another. In certain chapters I have opted for depth over breadth. I hope this will increase the book's readability. It may also help establish linkages between the economic, social, cultural, and political spheres, and thus stimulate critical thought, in ways that textbooks typically cannot.

Acknowledgements

A year spent as Visiting Professor at the Free University of Berlin in 1993-4 provided the opportunity to read widely and survey the German academic scene. For institutional support I am grateful to the Alexander von Humboldt Foundation, the FU Berlin, and the Historical Commission of Berlin. To Peter Steinbach in particular I owe a tremendous debt for his friendship and critical discussion. The following friends and colleagues deserve special thanks, as each of them read all or part of the manuscript at one stage or another: Lynn Abrams, John Breuilly, Timothy Brook, Roger Chickering, Richard J. Evans, Brett Fairbairn, Helen Graham, Thomas Kühne, and Stuart Robson. Others who sustained me during my travels in Germany include Johannes Hahn, Hans Horn, Gurli Jacobsen, Simone Lässig, Karl Heinrich Pohl, Wolfgang Schwentker, and the Schilfert family. To those who gave generously of their time, I promise I will now stop trying to referee the debate and 'get on with things'.

Research in Toronto would have been impossible without the assistance of Marline Otte and Richard Steigmann-Gall: they, like other students in my imperial Germany seminar since 1987, have enriched my outlook on the subject and forced me to clarify my thinking on many points. I am also pleased to acknowledge support from the Social Sciences and Humanities Research Council of Canada and the University of Toronto. To Gordon Martel I am grateful for permission to use material that appeared in another form in his edited collection, *Modern Germany Reconsidered*. Unless otherwise noted, all translations from German sources are my own, as are the graphics.

My children, Hanna and Stuart, have contributed in their own way to putting the study of Wilhelmine Germany in its proper perspective, though they have been forced to yield to the demands of the project too often. My greatest debt by far is to Helen Graham. To her this book is dedicated – undividedly.

The German Empire, 1871–1918

Prov. East Prussia

Prov. Pomerania

Prov. West Prussia

Prov. Poznań

Prov. Silesia

Kingdoms	Prussia
	Bavaria
	Saxony
	Württemberg
Grand Duchies	Baden
	Hessen
	Mecklenburg-Schwerin
	Mecklenburg-Strelitz
	Saxe-Weimar
	Oldenburg
Duchies	Brunswick
	Saxe-Meiningen
	Saxe-Altenburg
	Saxe-Coburg-Gotha
	Anhalt
Principalities	Schwarzburg-Sondershausen
	Schwarzburg-Rudolstadt
	Waldeck
	Reuss, older and younger lines
	Schaumburg-Lippe
	Lippe
Hansa cities	Lübeck
	Bremen
	Hamburg
Imperial Province	Alsace-Lorraine

——— Border of the German Empire

——— Border of a federal state

– – – – – Border of a Prussian province

P. Belonging to Prussia

O. Belonging to Oldenburg

M. Belonging to Mecklenburg-Strelitz

XV

Introduction

The Janus Face of Wilhelmine Germany

'I have been placed in an infinitely difficult period of history', Kaiser Wilhelm II told a confidant in 1903, requiring 'the reconciliation of traditional society with modern times' [142: p. 159]. Historians today are still grappling with the same problem that confronted Wilhelm. They are trying to reassess and reconcile lines of historical development that run through an epoch on the cusp of the twentieth century toward an ill-fated experiment in democracy, the triumph of fascism, genocide, division into two mutually antagonistic states and, ultimately, reunification. This book as a whole aims to show the reader that Wilhelmine Germany is coherent, meaningful, and comprehensible in its own right. Yet there is hardly another historical era that has been so rigorously analysed in negative terms: in terms, that is, not of what actually happened between 1888 and 1918 but of what happened *before* and *after*.

The 'before' story might seem relatively unproblematic. 'In the beginning was Bismarck' – this is how Thomas Nipperdey begins his account of German politics up to 1918 [192: vol. 2, p. 11]. But who came after Bismarck? Was Wilhelm II really the 'unperson' he appears to be in many accounts, and is his only important legacy that he lent his name to the Wilhelmine age? What about other Germans: How have historians viewed their hopes, their fears, their accomplishments, their failures? What did they inherit from Bismarck, what did they build anew, and what did they destroy? Under what constraints did they experience happiness and despair in their everyday lives? Answers to these questions are inevitably coloured by historians' assessments of the Bismarckian era. Between 1862 and his dismissal in 1890, Bismarck so dominated German politics at home and diplomacy abroad that his successors could not hope to measure up. Is it any wonder that German policy-making after 1890 appears so fractured in comparison with Bismarck's 'dictatorial' rule, or that the accelerating pace of change proved so unsettling to Wilhelmine Germans?

If Bismarck casts a long shadow on the Wilhelmine era specifically, the stain of Nazism on modern German history is longer still, and incomparably darker. For students, Wilhelmine Germany is exciting and interesting because it seems to be a dress-rehearsal for disaster – the disaster that befell Germany between 1933 and 1945. To be intrigued with possible continuities stretching from 1890 to 1945 is not to indulge in historical pathology, but rather to search for new and less well-trodden historical terrain where clues to later problems might be found. Although it is legitimate to ask whether this perspective necessarily provides insights into the larger sweep of German history, or whether it skews the questions we pose, the answer depends in great measure on the individual historian's willingness to embrace the open, contingent nature of history.

For example: German nationalism before 1914 can be seen as either benign or malignant, depending on what lines of development are believed to have led to National Socialism after 1933, to the new beginnings in East and West Germany after 1949, or to German reunification in 1990. German colonialism and imperialism can appear fairly typical in their European contexts; or they can be regarded as anticipating Hitler's expansionist program of mass deportations, the quest for *Lebensraum*, and world domination. German decisions in the July crisis of 1914 can be considered as merely one among many 'miscalculations' in the capitals of Europe; or they can be viewed within a larger pattern of German aggressiveness stretching back to Frederick the Great and up to Hitler's increasingly risky gambles between 1936 and 1945. Wilhelmine anti-Semitism remains controversial too. Did it reflect traditional religious prejudice? Or did it incorporate a dangerous new racial component that made it easier to contemplate mass extermination of the Jews? Lastly: What was truly unique about Germany's 'special path' (*Sonderweg*) to modernity? Did German history begin to go off the rails with the failure of the 1848 revolution and the subsequent decline of liberalism? Were the German middle classes incapable of playing the 'revolutionary' and 'emancipatory' roles played by corresponding groups

2

in Britain, France, and the United States? And did traditional German élites, fearful of losing their position, use their influence in the state, the military, and industry to unleash war, first in 1914 and again in 1939?

Today's generation of students can be excused for believing that the 'either–or' proposition found in some of these questions is still reflected in many standard historical accounts. They say you cannot tell a book by its cover. But the dustjackets of recent textbooks tend to depict two puzzlingly contradictory images of Wilhelmine Germany. One image is martial and threatening. The other is humane and benign. These contrasting images, moreover, seem to demand a choice between two quite distinct approaches to studying history. Those authors who believe that Bismarck dominated not only his own term of office but also Wilhelm's reign tend to favour traditional political history. This leads them to choose motifs for their dustjackets that depict the still-life of an authoritarian regime: a Prussian spiked helmet, a Bismarck monument, Wilhelm II wielding the sceptre of supreme command, or the Iron Chancellor gazing sadly into the chaotic future awaiting Germany after 1918. Other authors, however, choose very different images, based on their sympathy for a more eclectic mix of economic, social, intellectual, and cultural history. This Germany was dynamic, self-confident, and – at least relative to the standards of the age – surprisingly progressive. Here the appropriate symbols are the locomotive, the industrial factory, the bourgeois top hat, and the Modernist canvas. Over which Germany did Wilhelm II actually reign?

Principal Themes

In the 1990s, such mutually exclusive choices are no longer welcome. Nor do they represent the cutting edge of scholarship. This is as true for German history as it is for any other area of study. A central theme in what follows will be Wilhelmine Germany's Janus-faced character and its precarious position astride the nineteenth and twentieth centuries. The pace of social, economic, political, and cultural change after 1890 forced contemporaries to reflect on where they thought the young nation had struck root most

3

firmly, and where Germany's predicament in the new century seemed most insecure. For no group was this predicament of modernity more troubling than for the generation of youth born shortly after the unification of the Reich – that is, the generation reaching adulthood in the 1890s. Other developments, too, entered a new phase in the 1890s: Germany's second industrial revolution, the rise of mass politics, the women's movement, a Modernist revolt in the arts, and the abandonment of Bismarck's attempts to portray Germany as a 'satiated' power. Without ignoring lines of enquiry that carry the story backward and forward in time, in each case it is possible to examine the transitional nature of Wilhelmine developments in their own context.

This approach has necessitated a critical distancing from the *Sonderweg* concept – the interpretative model historians have used to suggest that German development from 1848 to 1945, for reasons to be explained in the following chapters, diverged from a 'normative' path leading to liberal democracy elsewhere in western Europe and culminated in the Nazi dictatorship of 1933–45. This book argues that the fate of Wilhelmine Germany was not predetermined either by a failure of German liberalism in 1848 or by Bismarck's political legacy. Moreover, the years 1888–1918 were not simply a staging-post leading directly to the stalemate of Weimar or the catastrophe of Nazism. This forces us to revise our understanding of authoritarianism, probably the best 'ism' to describe the political system of Wilhelmine Germany. Concentration on the Wilhelmine age allows us to explore the paradoxes of an authoritarian system of rule without simply equating it with 'Bismarckianism' or 'pre-fascism' in an uncritical way. On the level of everyday life too, Wilhelm's Germany was a fundamentally different place to live than Germany in the 1870s or the 1930s: Germans were more attuned to the tempo and opportunities of modern life than they had been in the age of Bismarck, but they were not yet willing to consider the 'total' solutions to their problems proposed by the Nazis. Germany's inheritance from Bismarck was unfortunate in innumerable ways, and it held within itself the seeds of later disasters. But the Wilhelmine age was not in any sense predestined to end in war and revolution, let alone the Third Reich. As one critic of the *Sonderweg* recently observed: 'Just like good show horses, historians should not jump their fences too early' [125: p. 344].

4

If one central theme of this book, then, concerns questions of historical continuity, a second theme is the contentiousness of the epoch itself: the fractured, conflict-ridden nature of Wilhelmine society and politics. For those Germans who were neither hopeless reactionaries nor dedicated revolutionaries, many issues of pressing public concern were difficult to confront squarely. As a result, political debate often revealed a surprising lack of consensus within individual classes, neighbourhoods, even families. We must therefore consider the multiple and overlapping identities of Germans in their full diversity – examining, for example, the different pressures on working-class Catholic fathers and middle-class Jewish mothers. Only in this way can we gain an accurate picture of what Wilhelmine Germany looked like from the 'inside'. This approach in turn will allow us to consider whether German society and politics were becoming pluralised or polarised before 1914. On the one hand, the idea of *social* cleavages will be introduced to consider whether German society was becoming more finely layered over time, or whether something might be salvaged from Marxist analyses postulating the division of society into two monolithic classes, one privileged and the other not. On the other hand we will also consider whether a polarisation of *political* forces occurred before 1914, leading to stalemate between opposing party blocs and the decision for war. What needs to be stressed here is that these two components – the social and the political – are interrelated parts of the 'pluralisation/polarisation' question. Conflict between social classes cannot be separated from the political threat posed by socialism. Similarly, the contemporary middle-class belief that men and women inhabited 'separate spheres' – the public sphere for men, the private sphere for women – was rooted in complex social patterns and in turn determined how power was wielded in state and society.

A third theme, developed throughout this study, is the geographical diversity of a state composed of twenty-five sovereign territories organised in a federal structure. Germany was not only a nation of urbanites living in huge metropolises. As Celia Applegate has suggested, it was also 'a nation of provincials' [11]. Up to 1918, local customs and habits of mind proved exceptionally resilient to pressures tending to amalgamate them into a uniform national culture. From a number of perspectives, Chapter 2 will consider the degree to which a liberal, middle-class, urban culture

5

failed to displace traditional mentalities and political allegiances in the countryside.

Organisation of the Book

To illuminate problems of historical interpretation and provide students with an overview, the four chapters have been organised to bring the analysis full circle in more than one sense. Chapter 1 outlines the major shifts in focus that have characterised the study of Wilhelmine Germany since 1945. Some dissatisfying generalisations about 'schools' of history are inevitable, for it is impossible to convey the full diversity of opinion *within* each 'school'. Yet establishing this interpretative framework will help the reader reach his or her own conclusions about issues raised in subsequent chapters.

Chapter 2 examines five principal developments. Changes in the economy and in social relations are discussed first. This lays the groundwork for an examination of how the Wilhelmine political system operated, how it changed, and the degree to which it was shaped by the efforts of parties and interest groups to mobilise a mass electorate. In the last two sections of the chapter, intellectual, religious, ethnic, and cultural developments are examined, as are issues of gender and sexuality. Chapter 3 shifts gears dramatically to examine current thinking about foreign policy. This chapter is briefer than the preceding one because Wilhelmine foreign policy, with the exception of the July crisis, has generally been less controversial than domestic policy. One might go further and suggest that the study of foreign policy has also generated less innovative scholarship.

Chapter 4 returns to a more interpretative format to examine the *many* Germanies of Wilhelm II. It takes up issues about class relations, first introduced in Chapter 2, and casts them in a new analytical light to reflect historiographical trends over the last thirty years: most notably, the trend away from the writing of history 'from above' to one that discusses historical change as driven by social and political forces acting both from above *and* from below. Chapter 4 also identifies points of scholarly divergence and consensus that have a larger significance for modern German history. The book's conclusions stress the vibrancy and promise of research currently being pursued in the archives.

In these pages the reader will be confronted with a sometimes dizzying array of historical viewpoints, where the interpretative 'switches' seem to be reversed every few years. Although these sudden reversals are often more apparent than real, it is true that historians must now contend with partial answers and unresolved paradoxes. Yet this situation need not induce panic or resignation. Instead it contributes to the excitement of making progress in historical study, just as the excitement of 'doing' science involves living with doubt and accepting that theories can never be proven, only disproven. In history as in science, the questions we pose change dramatically, often at an accelerating rate. At the same time, the sources and methods we use modify and illuminate older questions too. This book, in short, is as much about *how* we write history as about *what* we write.

1 Interpretative Turning Points

The Consensus of the 1950s

It is difficult now to imagine the outlook of the German historical profession after 1945. From the end of the Second World War until the early 1960s, most German scholars tended to argue that Hitler had come from nowhere to dupe the German people into supporting his regime [60: ch. 2; 112: pp. 17–23; 295]. Some historians, it is true, wanted to confront Germany's past. But conservatives in the profession, unwilling to address the Nazi catastrophe directly, advanced the notion of Hitler as an aberration, an unfortunate 'accident' of German history. This conviction in part explains why these historians laid the crimes of Nazism at the feet of an omnipotent state or ascribed Hitler's rise to power to a sudden twist of fate. As one account suggested: 'The Germans themselves were more surprised than anyone else by the rapid rise of the National-Socialist Party' [220: p. 381].

As a spokesman for this generation, Gerhard Ritter argued that the roots of Nazism stretched back no further than November 1918, after which an era of revolution, inflation, and depression led to the Nazi seizure of power. It was not in 1848, 1871, or 1890 that German history began to go off the rails, according to Ritter, but only after the First World War. This explanation of Nazism also suggested a particular interpretation of society and politics in Wilhelmine Germany. By ascribing Hitler's success to the rise of mass politics after 1918, Ritter and others suggested that up to that point the old ruling class had helped *defend* German politics against the vulgarity and self-interest of the masses. Only after November 1918, when politics was no longer conducted by local notables, was it possible for demagogues and party bureaucrats to thrive. By this reading, Germans had turned to Nazism not because liberal democracy failed but because Germany had become

8

too democratic. As Ritter wrote, neither Bismarck nor Wilhelm II were the forerunners of Hitler, but rather 'the demagogues and Caesars of modern history': Danton, Robespierre, Lenin, and Mussolini [220: p. 399].

Most German historians in the 1950s agreed on another point as well. They rejected the premise of Article 231 in the Treaty of Versailles, which asserted that Germany alone was responsible for the outbreak of war in 1914. Conservative historians believed instead that Europe as a whole had unwittingly 'slid' into war. Thus Germany bore no special blame. From this followed their insistence that no connection existed between German aggressiveness and German society before 1914. In fact these historians were scarcely concerned with the structure of society at all. Instead, history was the tale of how the state operated and what its leaders intended. This microscopic view of politics and diplomacy was too narrow to take in wider developments such as social dislocation, cultural anxiety, and political mobilisation before 1918. But it lent credence to the idea of Hitler as a sudden interloper.

The Fischer Controversy of the 1960s

Because this viewpoint was so widespread, it came as a tremendous shock to both academic and public opinion in Germany when the Hamburg historian Fritz Fischer produced the blockbuster book of 1961: eventually translated as *Germany's Aims in the First World War*, the original German title was more provocative, referring to Germany's *Bid for World Power* [76]. This meticulously researched monograph refuted the idea of Germany's innocence in the outbreak of war in 1914. It also inaugurated the acrimonious 'Fischer controversy', which dominated German historical discussion during the 1960s. Yet although Fischer set out to reconsider the aims of German foreign policy just before and during the war, in the long run he contributed more to revolutionising our thinking about German domestic politics for the entire period from 1871 to 1918 – and beyond [77; 78].

Fischer presented three main theses, some of which were fully developed only in his later books, and each of which is addressed

9

in Chapter 3. First, he argued that the German government in July 1914 accepted the risk that a major European war might result from its enthusiastic backing of Austria against Serbia after the assassination of Austrian Archduke Franz Ferdinand. Fischer subsequently radicalised this thesis to suggest that the Germans worked actively for war from 1912 onward. Second, Fischer illustrated that the annexationist war aims of the imperial government not only pre-dated the outbreak of war; they also shared a remarkable similarity with the Nazis' plans for foreign conquest after 1933. Third, he argued that the sources of aggressive expansionism were to be found less in Germany's international position than in its social, economic, and political situation at home. It was this third point, eagerly taken up first by Fischer's own students in Hamburg and then by a younger generation of German academics elsewhere, that changed writing about Wilhelmine Germany much more decisively than the war-aims debate itself.

According to this view, the seeds of German aggression in 1914 and 1939 could be found in the 1860s and 1870s. Unlike in other countries, where popular revolutions helped modernise states and societies, in Germany the imposition of authoritarian structures from above shaped the imperial constitution and the party system. Those structures, and the ruling élites who profited from them, were not flexible enough to adapt to the modern age. When tensions arising from rapid socio-economic change were incompletely deflected by those élites, aggressiveness was channelled outward, resulting in a drive for world-wide influence (*Weltpolitik*) and territorial expansion. Thus, Germany's unique misdevelopment at home in the nineteenth century explained its responsibility for twice unleashing war on Europe in the twentieth.

The 'Bielefelders' in the 1970s

When younger German historians set out to follow the impressive leads provided by Fischer and by neglected social historians of earlier eras, they produced a mountain of books so imposing that it can be reviewed only in outline. Among the most noteworthy contributions were Hans-Ulrich Wehler's analysis of Bismarck's imperialism [292; chs 5 and 15]; Jürgen Kocka's work on white-collar workers [Kocka in 112]; Hans-Jürgen Puhle's study of radical agrarianism [205]; Dirk Stegmann's analysis of parties and pressure groups [271]; Klaus Saul's [244] and Dieter Groh's [93] studies of relations between the labour movement, big industry, and the state; Imanuel Geiss's study of Wilhelmine foreign policy [90]; and Volker Berghahn's study of German naval construction [16]. When these and other authors contributed to an important collection of essays published in 1970, they revealed the degree to which attention had been refocused, in barely a decade, away from the 'accident' of Nazism onto the structures of authoritarianism in imperial Germany [276].

In 1973, the University of Bielefeld historian Hans-Ulrich Wehler realised the time had come to pull together the strands of this research and attempt a synthesis. Yet Wehler's study, later translated as *The German Empire 1871-1918*, only masqueraded as a textbook for students [291]. Its argument was intentionally critical and provocative. According to Wehler, imperial Germany was considerably more manipulative and brutish than it had appeared to Gerhard Ritter in the 1950s. Wehler was particularly uncompromising in condemning the willingness of the old ruling classes to protect their position by resorting to demagoguery and other weapons they found in the arsenal of mass politics. Modern propaganda, electoral chicanery, courtly ceremony, political indoctrination by school-teachers and drill sergeants – these were some of the techniques of rule Wehler identified as having affinities with the 'Bonapartist' strategies used by Emperor Napoleon III of France. In Germany, such techniques channelled ethnic, religious, and class hatreds into avenues designed to deflect revolution and perpetuate the traditional élites' enjoyment of privilege and power.

In Wehler's account, there was no doubt about where these élites received their political education: Bismarck designed and built the school-house of authoritarian rule. Thus Wilhelmine politics owed its immaturity to Bismarck's dictatorial determination to strangle the growth of democratic institutions. Wilhelmine diplomacy owed its restless spirit to the militarism heightened during Bismarck's wars of unification in the 1860s. Wilhelmine society owed its willingness to discriminate against minorities to Bismarck's campaigns against 'enemies of the Reich'. And

11

Wilhelmine industrial capitalism, despite its rapid efflorescence, served only the interests of heavy-industrial employers and agrarians.

The unity of perspective between Wehler and Fischer is clear, despite their different methods and their disagreement on particular points. Fischer wrote in his second major book, *War of Illusions* (1969), that the aim of German policy between 1911 and 1914 was 'to consolidate the position of the ruling classes with a successful imperialist foreign policy'. A war, it was hoped, 'would resolve the growing social tensions' [77: p. viii]. Moreover, both historians agreed that when the tensions seething beneath the surface of Wilhelmine Germany finally broke through, the effect was all the more devastating because the delaying tactics of anti-democratic élites had been so successful. The reckless gamble of 1914 exploded in 1918 – and in 1933. Because Wilhelmine élites had evaded political reform so long, Germany and Europe paid the price many times over.

By the mid-1970s no one could dispute the splash Wehler had made with his *German Empire* book. Yet the different labels historians attached to the outlook he championed reveal that it was neither understood in a uniform way nor accepted uncritically [172; 215; 224; 295]. For some, the label 'Bielefeld school' seemed appropriate because three Bielefeld professors (Wehler, Kocka, and Puhle) took the lead in defending the new position. Yet their views found sympathisers outside Bielefeld too. For other historians, there were at least four reasons to describe this as a 'critical social science': (i) because it was critical of both imperial German authoritarianism and the historiographical traditions that had so long denied its significance; (ii) because it pursued political and pedagogical goals designed to make the writing of modern German history more relevant to a new generation of students ('1968ers') questioning established values; (iii) because it deliberately cultivated interdisciplinary contacts with sociology, political science, and related fields; and (iv) because it stressed the fruitfulness of considering German developments in a comparative perspective. The label 'structural history' seemed appropriate, too, for the emphasis fell not on the role of individuals, or even on individual policies and decisions, but rather on the underlying structures of history. For a time the label 'Kehrites' came into vogue, highlighting Wehler's effort to resurrect the works of

Eckart Kehr, Hans Rosenberg, and other social historians [132; Rosenberg in 112; 240; Mommsen in 258]. Lastly, the assertion that the 'Bielefelders' embraced a 'social history of politics' or a 'new social history' suggested, rightly, that their brand of social history was more relevant to political historians than economic, social, and quantitative history in their traditional forms.

Although the term 'new orthodoxy' was used as early as the mid-1970s to describe the influence of the group around Wehler, nothing resembling a new orthodoxy ever monopolised German historical opinion. Even though the 'Bielefelders' saw themselves working for change in what had been, in their view, a monolithic profession, they remained a minority. Wehler's *German Empire* book encountered withering criticism as soon as it was published, and many deemed his account so one-sided as to be implausible [88: p. 7; 153; 190: ch. 15; 300]. As Chapter 3 will demonstrate, well-established diplomatic historians levelled their own critiques against the 'primacy of domestic policy' approach. In any case, acceptance of the 'Bielefeld' position was never an all-or-nothing proposition [e.g. the mix of viewpoints in 51; 112; 258; 276]. Certainly Wilhelmine historiography was given a decisive impetus by the prolific Bielefeld workshop; but one can argue that the field has been enriched just as decisively by historians who have taken on board some features of Wehler's portrait, rejected others, and suggested alternative explanations of their own [e.g. 175, 224: pp. 40–2, 50–1; 227: intro.]. East German scholarship prior to 1989, although restricted by political orthodoxy of another sort, complemented the work of scholars in the Federal Republic – for example, through local studies of peasant farming in the fertile *Börde* region around Magdeburg [49; Plaul et al. in 68]. Lastly, neither the Bielefeld group nor their critics have stood still [e.g. 138; 296]. Jürgen Kocka, before leaving for the Free University of Berlin, was instrumental in leading the large bourgeoisie study at the University of Bielefeld, discussed in Chapter 4. Any day now the next instalment of Wehler's mammoth 'history of society' (*Gesellschaftsgeschichte*) is due to appear, dealing with the period 1848–1914 [294]. Until it does, Nipperdey's two-volume history of imperial Germany, published in 1990–2, will stand as the closest thing we have to an '*histoire totale*' of this period [192]. But – again, all to the good – even this volume has been greeted with a mixed reception [e.g. 66].

Revision of the Revisionists

Just as Wehler's synthesis gave a measure of coherence to the research conducted in the late 1960s and early 1970s, sceptics of Wehler's model owe much to a comprehensive statement of purpose that appeared at another critical stage of debate. This time the call was answered by a British historian, Richard J. Evans, who in 1978 edited a volume of essays that brought together a group of younger British historians with a viewpoint quite different from Wehler's [67]. These historians, too, disagreed with the older conservative historiography. However, they thought Wehler and other 'Bielefelders' had gone too far in stressing the degree of social control exercised by élites. Shifting their focus down to the level of ordinary people, they found not puppets and dupes of authoritarian stage-managers dancing toward the final curtain of the Third Reich, but historical actors who responded ambivalently and unpredictably to convulsive forces of change.

The following chapters showcase different aspects of the new research keeping Wilhelmine scholarship alive and innovative. At the end of Chapter 4 we take stock of the current 'state of the art' in the field. David Blackbourn's and Geoff Eley's book, *The Peculiarities of German History*, also discussed in Chapter 4, played a key role in prompting a reassessment of the German *Sonderweg* during the 1980s [24]. At this point it is the highly *eclectic* character of recent work that needs to be emphasised. What factors are responsible for this eclecticism? Clearly, postmodernism has contributed to a proliferation of theoretical and methodological approaches. Here the 'new cultural history' has made a decisive contribution in redirecting attention toward mentalities, experiences, identities, and cultural environments at all levels of society [36; 57]. Feminist history and gender history have also begun to exert a strong influence in the field. Some of this work remains largely theoretical or preliminary, and some of it fails to apply theory to practice in entirely convincing ways [see e.g. Chickering's scepticism in 197]. Yet empirical work based on a pluralism of methods has now been underway long enough for its findings to be assimilated by a wide audience. The opening up of archives in the former East Germany (GDR) is already sending a new generation of scholars toward sources that will prompt a reconsideration of old orthodoxies. A recent study of the practice of civil liberties in such far-flung territories as Baden, Bavaria, Prussia, and Saxony is but one of many examples where improved access to state archives in eastern Germany is dramatically changing our estimate of how national legislation was actually implemented at the local level [143; also 87; 148].

Admittedly, there remain formidable institutional barriers to overcome if this reinvigoration of scholarship is to continue. With world-wide economies still in disarray, non-European doctoral students are often unable to afford the long archival visits their elders once took for granted. Within Germany itself, social tension, high unemployment, and the restructuring of university faculties in the former GDR have rendered scholarly dialogue between eastern and western scholars more muted than anyone predicted in 1990. These problems suggest that historians working away at the cutting edge of Wilhelmine scholarship will require diligence and increased institutional support. Even if this happens, there is little likelihood that a more systematic research agenda will emerge: paradigms, approaches, and angles of interest change too quickly for the gaps identified by one generation to retain their interest for the next. Whereas some observers are convinced that the most exciting work currently underway is on the early-modern, Nazi, or post-1945 periods, others believe that imperial Germany attracts many of the best talents. Whatever the case, the broad front on which work is being conducted is an exciting development in its own right. Today hardly anyone would deny that the Wilhelmine era remains a frontier where critically important insights into other periods of German history remain to be discovered.

2   The Birth of the Modern Age

The Changing Economy

From agrarian to industrial state

Wilhelmine Germany has been compared to a busy anthill, its population always at work, always on the move [102: p. 160]. Between 1888 and 1914, the German population rose from just under 50 million to almost 68 million persons. By the mid-1890s, the mammoth wave of emigration that characterised the 1880s had effectively dried up. Internal migration meanwhile continued unabated after 1890. It was among the most important factors accelerating the growth of cities. Younger, often unmarried persons travelled great distances from the underdeveloped areas in Prussia's eastern provinces to the large industrial centres of central and western Germany, most notably to Saxony and the Ruhr district [14].

The proportion of the workforce employed in the three principal economic sectors also shifted dramatically. The number of Germans employed in agriculture, forestry, and fishing (the primary sector) increased moderately over this period. Yet the number employed in industry and handicrafts (the secondary sector) increased far more rapidly, as did those in trade, commerce, and transportation (the tertiary sector). Figure 2.1 illustrates these trends. The overlaid arrow indicates that sometime around 1900 the blocs representing agriculture and industry were close to equal. The outcome, however, had been decided long before the turn of the century [15; 168]. The direction and magnitude of these population shifts are even

16

more apparent if we consider not just employed persons but these *and* their family dependents in each category – that is, the total number of people who depended on one sector or the other for their livelihood. By this reckoning, between 1882 and 1907 the proportion of Germans dependent on agriculture fell from 42 to 28 per cent. Those dependent on industry and crafts rose from 35 to 42 per cent, and those dependent on trade, commerce, and transportation rose from 9 to 13 per cent [107: p. 66].

The proportions that agriculture, industry, and trade and commerce contributed to Germany's net national product (NNP) also shifted decisively (see Figure 2.2). In 1888 the contributions of agriculture on the one hand, and industry, mining, and handicrafts on the other hand, were about equal. By 1913, agriculture's share of NNP had sunk to less than one-quarter, whereas the secondary sector was approaching one-half. In other words, industry had emerged as the undisputed engine of change in the economy, pulling all other sectors along as it rode the upward curve.

It is worth noting that although German agriculture was not on the ropes before 1914, agriculture's relative share of economic output did decline markedly. The absolute value of agricultural production rose over 42 per cent between 1888 and 1913. Most of this rise occurred after 1895. Many individual calamities notwithstanding, German agriculture was in no danger of disappearing. Nevertheless, German agricultural producers after the 1880s faced growing competition from producers in Argentina, Australia, Canada, and the United States, who benefited from improved storage, refrigeration, and transportation facilities. These trends contributed to a steady long-term decline in commodity prices and to other structural factors commonly associated with industrialisation: the extraction of wealth from agriculture; the depopulation of many rural regions; shifts from extensive (grain) farming to intensive (cattle and pig) farming; and the resurgence of peasant agriculture supported by co-operative movements. As we shall see, these factors contributed to social protectionism and the political mobilisation of rural voters, thereby ensuring that the alleged crisis of German agriculture remained a topic of intense political debate.

17

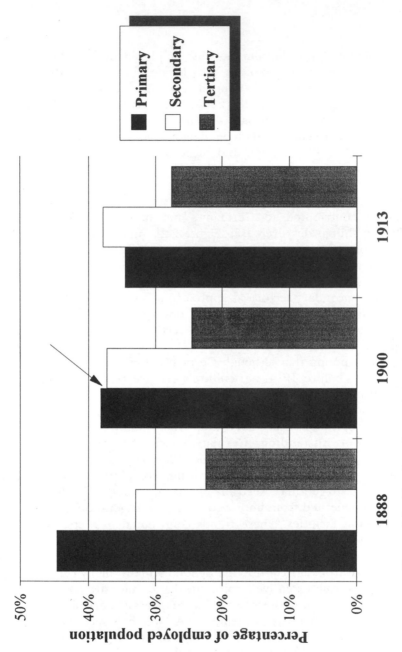

Figure 2.1 Employed population, by economic sector, 1888–1913.
Source: [106: p. 205].

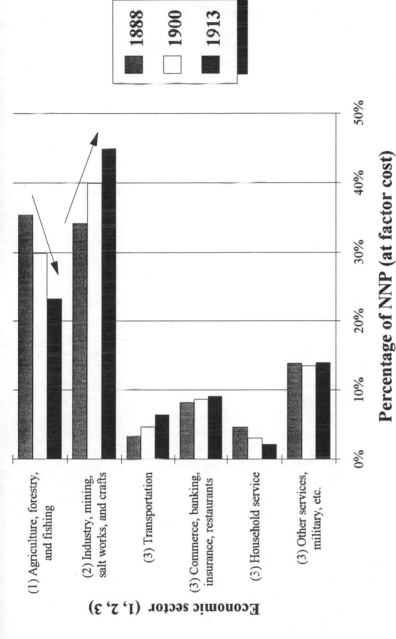

Figure 2.2 Share of net national product, by economic sector, 1888–1913.
Source: [106: pp. 454–5].

19

Wilhelm II ascended the throne near the midpoint of a temporary upswing (1886–90) in the economy. There soon followed a sharp downturn in prices, investments, and interest rates (1891–4). Then from 1895 to 1913 rapid growth was fuelled by unprecedentedly high rates of investment and by steady increases in the value of both exports and imports [107: pp. 85–6]. Although still afflicted by short downturns, most notably those of 1900–2 and 1907–8, this was imperial Germany's most sustained economic 'boom'. There were no real 'busts'.

It is important to see periodic upturns and downturns in the larger context of virtually uninterrupted productive growth over the period 1888–1914. This helps resolve a dispute between two groups of historians: those who emphasise the significance of the so-called 'Great Depression' of 1873–96, and those who argue that in fact no depression occurred at all. Two viewpoints can be cited as representative of the first body of opinion. Long ago Hans Rosenberg called attention to the social, political, psychological, and diplomatic repercussions of economic depression after 1873 [Rosenberg in 258]. According to Rosenberg, many features of post-1873 politics are understandable only in terms of economic dislocation and uncertainty. These features include interest-group agitation, anti-Semitism, and the wish to divert social tensions abroad through nationalism and imperialism. Subsequently, Hans-Ulrich Wehler, Volker Berghahn, and others examined 'social imperialism' as a strategy that combined attempts to overcome uneven economic growth with efforts to legitimise political domination. In their view social imperialism was based mainly on German capitalists' desperate wish for an 'anti-cyclical therapy'. This therapy would provide new markets, alleviate irregular or retarded growth, stabilise the constitutional structure at home, and distract workers from their lowly status. However – still following this line of argument – when periodic downturns occurred, they provided 'painful reminders that there was no such thing as a continuous and even rise in economic development'. As a result, leaders of industry complained in the same breath about 'low prices' and 'impertinent workers' [Berghahn and Wehler in 112, esp. p. 206; 54: chs 2, 5, and 6].

The current consensus among historians suggests that these economic explanations cannot bear the interpretative weight loaded upon them. It may be true that Germans *perceived* short-term downturns as misfortunes. These perceptions, even if false, may have helped shape the political mood of the times. But the extreme regional and sectoral unevenness of economic development argues against any uniform political reaction, as does the diversity of ways in which suffering was actually experienced by specific groups. Most economic 'downturns' were actually just periods of slower economic growth, not of actual contraction. Therefore many historians would point to the fact that the annual growth rate averaged approximately 4.5 per cent for the period 1890–1913 – an achievement most leaders of industrialised countries today would envy. Crises in the industrial sector, therefore, now seem less important than the technological and structural innovations that marked the beginning of Germany's second industrial revolution [30; 31: p. 135; 99: p. 205; Born in 258].

A good example of such innovation was the first successful transmission of electrical current in 1891 over a distance of 175 km from Lauffen to Frankfurt on Main. This may be said to have launched the German electrical industry. In 1891 the production of electricity contributed only about 45 million marks to the German economy. By 1913 that figure had risen to 1.3 billion marks. Electricity is a 'flexible' commodity – easily transported, convertible into light, heat, or power, and switched on or off in an instant. It therefore proved instrumental in bringing new sources of power to large factories and deep mineshafts, to small workshops and isolated farmyards, to city streets and individual households. In a similar way the spin-offs from the new petrochemical industries had great impact. They heightened Germany's industrial presence internationally. As well as leading in the production of certain heavy chemicals, in pharmaceuticals, and in products derived through electrochemical means, Germany produced over 90 per cent of the world's synthetic dyes by 1900. Long before 1914 German exports had penetrated into virtually all geographic and sectoral niches once dominated by the British. This prompted a 'trade envy' among the latter that only backfired when British consumers insisted on the famous 'Made in Germany' label.

The giant electrical and chemical enterprises that led this second industrial revolution are now household names: Siemens,

AEG, Bayer, BASF, Hoechst, and Schering. What is less commonly known is that these firms were among the first in the world to demonstrate the benefits of intensive scientific research. Conducted by scientists and technicians working both in university laboratories and 'in-house', this research could be applied directly to the production of traditional consumer items, to the development of new ones (for example, the automobile and the telephone), and to meeting the growing requirements of public works [124]. Figure 2.3 demonstrates that growth in the number of employees in the electrochemical sector outstripped that in most other sectors. There were other characteristically modern innovations in industrial organisation. Among the most important of these were the following: (i) The development of top managerial positions and expertise. Chief executive officers – for instance, Alfred Hugenberg at Krupp – replaced first- and second-generation owners as hands-on managers, often rivalling them in power. (ii) Horizontal and vertical concentration of industries. This permitted producers' monopolies to set production quotas and prices, or to streamline production from the pithead to the end of the assembly line. (iii) A new relationship between industries and banks, allowing representatives of the banks to sit on industrial boards to protect their financial investments. (iv) Larger workforces in individual enterprises. Small workshops by no means disappeared. But whereas about 60 per cent of those employed in industry and handicrafts worked in enterprises with five or fewer employees in 1882, by 1907 only 31 per cent fell into this category [18: ch. 3; 31; 106: p. 212].

It would be wrong to imagine that the second industrial revolution bore no resemblance to the first. The classic heavy industries of mining and steel production remained extremely important even after 1890. The rapidly expanding need for specialised components, precision tools, and finely calibrated measuring instruments also continued to fuel the metalworking industry. Nevertheless, the more conspicuous rise of white-collar workers and professionals illustrates that the tertiary sector was gaining in importance. As local governments became increasingly complex and proactive, the number of civil servants (*Beamten*) grew enormously [147; 239; 257; 273]. Associated trades, for example the legal profession and health services, benefited directly. The commercial sector, too, required vastly increased numbers of

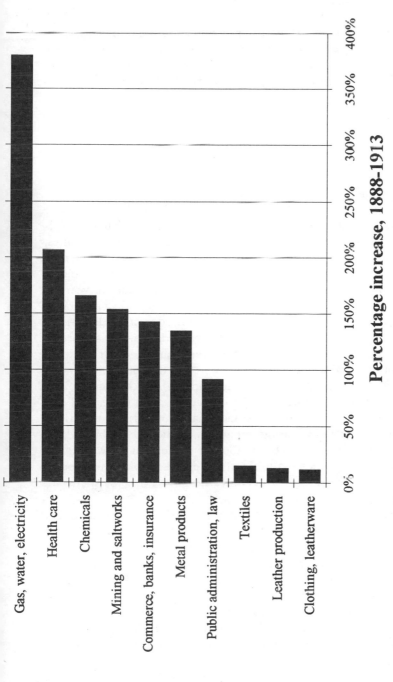

Figure 2.3   Increase in number of persons employed in selected occupations, 1888–1913.
Source: [106: pp. 196–201].

white-collar workers. Thus, as a percentage of the total workforce, there was a steep rise of salaried employees (*Angestellten*) – those who were neither independent owner-operators nor worked for a daily wage [107: pp. 69–71; Kocka in 112; Kocka in 276].

Social Inequalities and Urbanism

Winners and losers in capitalist development

Understanding how German capitalism changed structurally is only the first step toward assessing its impact on society, politics, and culture. One's perception of economic well-being not only depended on whether the economy was expanding as a whole. It also depended on whether it was buoyant or stagnant this year (or this week); on whether employment could be found on a particular farm or shopfloor; and on whether one lived in a locality where national patterns of prosperity were reproduced. These factors determined how economic 'realities' were translated into political perceptions, and when perceptions were acted upon (for example, when strikes erupted and when they did not). By the same token, the economic acrobatics we use to determine real wages and real prices should not disguise the fact that short-term fluctuations sometimes had a devastating impact on the household budgets of German workers. As one farm labourer wrote: 'Oh, how beautiful and heavy every taler [equivalent to 3 marks] looks when you've earned it, and how light it becomes when you have to spend it!' [133: p. 193].

It took some time for historians to reach a consensus about whether real wages for workers rose or fell during the Wilhelmine era. Older studies suggested that real wages stagnated after 1900. According to this view, although productivity increased and nominal wages rose, the cost of living rose even more quickly. Thus the real purchasing power of workers shrank [34]. Newer research suggests the opposite conclusion. Taking into account a broader range of consumer items and sources of income than early studies did, we find that the impact of rising prices is diminished [46].

24

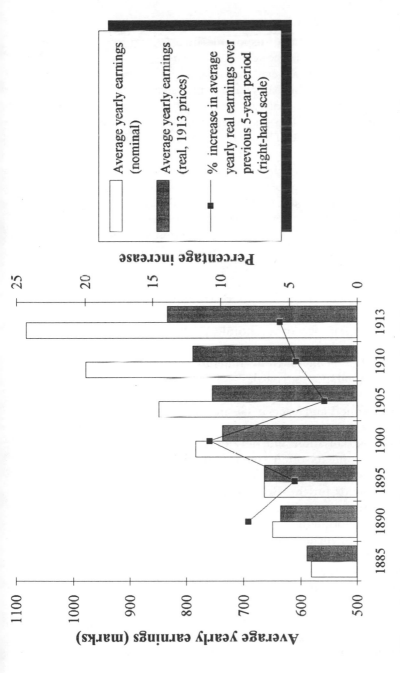

Figure 2.4 Average yearly earnings (nominal and real) for employees in industry, trade, and transportation, 1885–1913.

Source: [107: p. 107; based on 46: pp. 112–25].

Previous estimates of real disposable income and its purchasing power, therefore, should be revised upwards.

Figure 2.4 shows changes in nominal and real wages for certain industrial sectors. The bar chart demonstrates the divergence between nominal and real earnings. Yet the overlaid line graph demonstrates the considerable fluctuation in the *rate* whereby real earnings rose over time. The increase in real wages between 1895 and 1900 is especially noteworthy – almost 11 per cent. The short, severe downturn after 1900 is equally apparent. Yet the reader should note that annual percentage increases never dipped below zero. For the overall period 1885–1913, real wages are believed to have risen over 31 per cent. This was at a time when unemployment rarely exceeded 3 per cent and when the length of the average workweek was falling – from over 70 hours in the late 1870s to 54–60 hours shortly before the war [30; 97; 192: vol. 1, p. 302]. In short, the smoothness of the longer trend belies the volatility of the shorter ones. This discrepancy reveals that actual economic achievement is not necessarily consistent with contemporaries' experience of economic performance. It also helps explain why early historians erroneously extrapolated evidence of a boom-or-bust economy from contemporary accounts that tended to be anecdotal, not statistical.

Because there are so many ways to draw up the balance sheet between winners and losers in German industrialisation, sharp differences of interpretation still come to the fore. Historians who study industrialisation and development in European and non-European contexts often stress that the key point is less the movement of wages than the larger disruption of society. This observation holds for the German case too. When people moved from rural communities to find higher wages in the cities, they often lost important non-monetary benefits of country life. These benefits might include seemingly minor goods such as produce from a small garden plot or milk from a goat; they could also include larger social support systems and a clean environment. Although these advantages of living in the countryside were not reflected in wage levels, they made a material difference to people's lives. Urban workers generally earned higher wages once they arrived in the big city, but many were actually worse off in all ways that really mattered.

It is hardly surprising that those historians who wish to stress the discriminatory and inegalitarian nature of Wilhelmine society tend to focus on the *dis*advantages that economic modernisation brought to the working classes. This viewpoint characterised much of the economic history written in the former East Germany. In this work, even though the German bourgeoisie was seen as subordinating its interests to those of the 'feudal' Junkers who owned grain-growing estates in the Prussian east, capitalist exploitation and the drive for imperialist and colonial expansion overseas were seen as impeding the achievement of fair productive relationships at home [49: ch. 6]. But among West German historians no such consensus emerged. Some historians still suggest that we cannot calculate the benefits and liabilities of industrialisation on a national level at all [99: pp. 62–81; 196; 282]. Others emphasise that the contours of industrial expansion illustrate much of what was good about life in Wilhelmine Germany. German society, they argue, was no more unfair in the distribution of wealth than other European societies, and all classes benefited from industrial expansion [e.g. 192: vol. 1, ch. 6].

These questions have led to studies of social mobility and social stratification that are considerably more nuanced than in the 1970s. Summing up these findings, Volker Berghahn recently posed two key questions: Was the class make-up of Wilhelmine society finely textured, and perhaps becoming more so over time? Or were class blocs emerging with 'recognizably bolder dividing lines'? [18: p. 50] These questions will be considered further in Chapter 4. At this point it is sufficient to note that most newer studies agree that German industrialisation had three important social consequences. Each of these points might appear surprising at first, but only if one assumes that growth should be equated with social progress and wages with well-being. Instead one can argue that German development was *not* as unique as the *Sonderweg* concept would suggest in highlighting the unfortunate political implications of rapid socio-economic change. Put another way, the real surprise may be that the rapid and uneven nature of German industrialisation was a fairly typical path toward modernisation after all.

The first point is that there does *not* appear to have been a significant overall increase in social mobility between classes [107: p. 98]. Very few sons or daughters of workers managed to claw their way into the ranks of the bourgeoisie, largely because they had

27

virtually no access to higher education. Somewhat more vertical upward mobility occurred between the lower-middle and the upper-middle classes. Yet the lower-middle classes tended to move horizontally in crab-like fashion or ascended slowly over two or three generations [22: ch. 5]. Important distinctions of privilege also separated the middle classes from the nobility.

Second, the inequalities of wealth and income between the upper and upper-middle classes on the one hand, and the lower-middle and lower classes on the other hand, appear to have *increased*, not diminished. The real wages of workers and the incomes of shopkeepers and artisans improved markedly. But the sources of income more typical of the upper and upper-middle classes – salaries, pensions, and dividends – rose even more steeply [230: p. 150]. Among workers, incomes between different categories of earners appear to have *diverged* rather than converged. Differentials expanded between skilled and unskilled workers and between males and females. These trends only heightened contemporary perceptions of unequal opportunity.

Third, regional economic disparities appear to have *increased* rather than decreased over time. This conclusion goes against the grain of many assumptions about the economic achievement inherent in national unification. It suggests that the national economy was not becoming homogenised, even under the impact of advances in communication and transportation that favoured the emergence and exploitation of national markets. Quite the contrary: disparity was created by industrialisation, not by the lack of it. Regional unevenness increased precisely because these factors were tying the country as a whole into a national economy but at the same time facilitating concentrations of productive capacity and specialisation among regions. Thus the 'indexes of specialisation' one economic historian devised for each region of Germany show a strong correlation between rapid global change and increasing economic specialisation [282: esp. pp. 87–8; also 30: ch. 3]. Germany in 1913 had many regions where underdevelopment stood out more conspicuously than ever before. Although these were not necessarily the same economic backwaters as in 1871, the agrarian, depopulated, 'have-not' provinces of eastern Prussia were falling behind the national average, while the urbanised, industrial regions of central and western Germany were pulling ahead.

Thus far we have seen that winners and losers in German industrialisation are difficult to classify unless we consider economic sector and geographic origin. Another complicating factor is that barriers dividing rural and urban society were becoming more permeable. As Figure 2.5 illustrates, massive demographic shifts reduced the proportion of Germans living in small towns and villages with fewer than 2000 inhabitants and increased the proportion living in large cities. These figures do not speak to the problem of gauging the *qualitative* changes in the lives of city dwellers. 'No statistic can mirror the grotesque things that happen in the expanding cities', wrote one urban reformer in 1899; 'no imagination can picture the most remarkable individual cases' [231: p. 56]. In fact there is almost no limit to the imagination with which scholars have begun to document the misery of urban life during Wilhelm's reign. We are now well attuned to the close correlation between desperate material circumstances and susceptibility to the hazards of big-city life. Conversely, studies of bourgeois civic pride have also revealed the narrowness of the social stratum that felt truly at home in these rapidly changing urban environments [Lees and Merkl in 51; 62; Pogge von Strandmann in 125; 147; Pohl in 148; 264].

There is no way here to reflect the full range of contemporary reactions to urban living, either positive or negative. But perhaps one vignette can illustrate why historians are now interested in exploring Wilhelmine Germans' ambivalent reactions to urbanism as a reflection of more subtle changes in everyday mentalities. Extrapolating from an account of an unlucky afternoon spent in Berlin's giant Wertheim department store, written in 1903 by an aristocrat named Fedor von Zobeltitz, one gains a sense of such ambivalence [231: pp. 108–9].

It was a matter [wrote von Zobeltitz] of purchasing an assortment of items that my wife said were better and cheaper at Wertheim's (though her tone put the emphasis on 'cheaper'). . . . First I tried to get my bearings. I don't easily get lost, but here my topographical talents abandoned me altogether. The streaming mass of humanity pushed me this way and that; I wanted to get to the perfumes and ended up in hard-

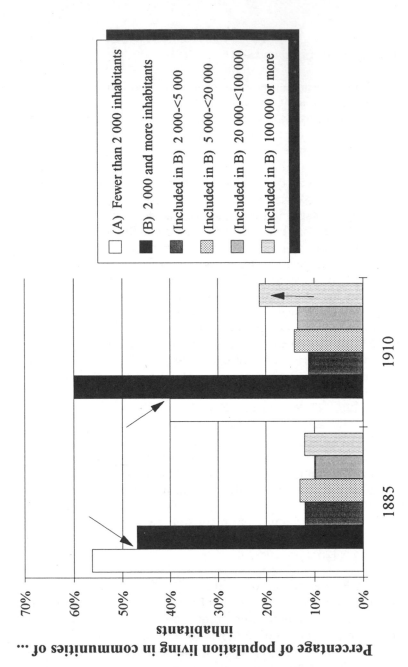

Figure 2.5 Distribution of population by size of community, 1885–1910.
Source: [107: p. 52].

Legend:
- (A) Fewer than 2 000 inhabitants
- (B) 2 000 and more inhabitants
- (Included in B) 2 000–<5 000
- (Included in B) 5 000–<20 000
- (Included in B) 20 000–<100 000
- (Included in B) 100 000 or more

Percentage of population living in communities of ... inhabitants waie, then suddenly I was standing in front of a woman showing me handkerchiefs, and a half-minute latei I had stumbled onto enameled utensils. . . .

One of the official guides, a man who looked like a diplomatic undersecretary, told me I should use the elevator or the escalator. . . . This I proceeded to do; . . . but I found myself in a painting exhibit. . . . A man who looked like a privy councillor from the Ministry of Culture could see my embarrassment and asked me what I was looking for. 'Up', he said, smiling, and pointed to the elevator. But I hadn't paid attention: the elevator was going down, not up – and when I looked around I was in a magnificent hall with lapis-lazuli columns and a roaring fountain.

This was getting a bit tiresome. I pressed on with weary steps, came to a palm garden and a buffet where a cute little girl presented me with a glass of lemonade, next I was into a muddle of children's garments . . . then to the phonographs and finally to the perfumes I was looking for. Thank God – at last!

City dwellers often judged their immediate environments according to yardsticks taken from their former surroundings, whether this be their former place of residence, frequently the countryside, or a different socio-economic milieu. This may explain the combination of excitement and dismay we discern in Zobeltitz's account. After all, this particular nobleman is disoriented precisely because he *is* noble: finding himself in a sham aristocratic setting designed to appeal to bourgeois tastes, the upper-crust Zobeltitz gets muddled by the commercial *trompe l'oeil*. This prompts two further observations. The first is that the Wilhelmine debate about commercialism, consumerism, and luxury was almost exclusively a middle-class phenomenon. As such it displayed the bourgeois tendency to try to *control* change, or to manage it, rather than reject it across the board [32]. This tendency was reflected in Werner Sombart's study of *Luxury and Capitalism* (1913) and even in Paul Göhre's study of the Wertheim department store itself. In these and similar works, German culture (*Kultur*) was viewed as under siege: wealth and luxury, having corrupted civilisation (*Zivilisation*) in Rome and France, now threatened Central Europe. In these accounts the department store, situated firmly within the urban milieu, represented a multitude of other bourgeois anxieties. These anxieties included the fear of overspending or otherwise overstepping one's capacities (because one could browse as long as one liked); the negative effect of diplaying luxurious goods to all classes, particularly when those lacking education or cultivation (*Bildung*) could shop in the same venues as the higher born (thus Wertheim shop clerks were instructed to preserve the anonymity of persons of high standing when a 'simpler person' was within earshot); the creation of new and indefensible public spaces; and the alleged inability of women to resist either enticements to purchase or temptations to shoplift. As Warren Breckman has pointed out, the debate about luxury revealed how disconcerting the German bourgeoisie found modernity in general [32].

The second point is that the discreet charm of rural life was often placed in false opposition to the alleged corruption of the big city. Critics of the city, whose views dominated the early literature on German anti-modernism, equated urban life with the atomisation of society and with such out-groups as Jews and the 'reds' [156; 274]. Of course the charm of the countryside was largely mythical, as Germany's long history of rural anti-Semitism reveals. And what charm there was certainly did not remain inviolate. The distance to the city, whether measured in social or cultural terms, was shrinking rapidly. Nevertheless, many Germans persisted in feeling that rural life was somehow (and forever) 'different'. Even though Karl Marx dismissed the distinctive cultural touchstones of the countryside as part of 'the idiocy of rural life', his disdain has not prevented them from shaping experiences and mentalities up to the present day.

In the end, negative images of the urban metropolis are of little help in explaining why so many migrants voted with their feet and flocked to the huge cities – or why, once they had 'arrived' (in whatever sense), at least *some* of them found urban life exhilarating. Undifferentiated critiques of the big city are even less helpful in illuminating those features of urban life in which historians are currently most interested. These include occupational profiles, labour markets, and employer–employee relations; problems of housing, sanitation, health, and nutrition; the role of generational cohorts; environmental and lifestyle reform movements; and links between Germans' civic pride and the fate of liberalism, Jewish culture, and bourgeois manners [e.g. Kleßmann in 14; 45; 48; 62;

123; 193]. Taken together, these issues still confront historians with a wide array of questions awaiting answers. How did migrants from the countryside interact with those already living in cities? Did the promise of anonymity translate into a kind of *de facto* social equality? Did it foster class consciousness instead? Or did it, as urban critics claimed, feed only political apathy and moral irresponsibility? Did cities actually 'create' urban crime? Were cities the only places where avant-garde art could thrive? Were Germans trying to deny the national distinctiveness of their urban culture when they insisted on calling Berlin 'Athens on the Spree' and Dresden 'Florence on the Elbe'?

Answers to these questions will undoubtedly continue to draw upon contemporary observations like those provided by the popular lecturer and sociologist Georg Simmel, who postulated that city dwellers were afflicted by a kind of 'daily civil war of sense impressions'. Peter Jelavich has taken up this lead in suggesting that cabaret was a symptomatic cultural manifestation of urban life. Offering crass commercialism, blatant self-promotion, and the momentary sensation all rolled into one, cabaret's fast pace and fragmented nature neatly reproduced the open-ended forms of Modernist culture: it fascinated audiences impatient with tradition, patrons weary of 'closure'. To be sure, the slice-of-life drama, the philosophical aphorism, the Post-Impressionist canvas frozen in time – these were distinctive features of Wilhelmine culture along with the 'vaudeville style'. Yet the following passage suggests that the larger symbolism Jelavich sees in cabaret and Breckman sees in conspicuous consumption was not lost on contemporaries. When a Berlin variety show lampooned the metropolis as a giant department store, the commodities on display were fashioned to suit every taste and activity [119: p. 116].

Customer: Politics!
               Employee: To the right, please!
Customer: Municipal affairs!
               Employee: To the left, please!
Customer: Something dramatic!
               Employee: Right here, please! . . .
Customer: Fashion and sports!
               Employee: Proceed to the first floor . . . !

Customer: Courtroom!
        Employee: Second floor.
Customer: City gossip!
        Employee: Third floor.

The Authoritarian State and Mass Politics

Revolution or reform? The state and the rule of law

It is tempting to view Wilhelmine Germany as a house divided against itself. On one side stands the repressive, authoritarian state, determined to marginalise all non-conformist groups within society, dismissive of the force of public opinion, and ready for battle on every front. On the other side stand the political parties, lobby groups, and voluntary associations which, collectively and often despite themselves, represent pressures for change emanating from German society. Such pressures may be the result of conflicting material interests, antagonistic social relations, or political aspirations for reform. In any case, these organisations operate in a 'civil liberties environment' where basic constitutional rights – the legally guaranteed freedoms of expression, of the press, of association, and of assembly – are institutionalised as part of a 'public sphere' (*Öffentlichkeit*). Standing outside the direct control of the state, though not always in opposition to it, the public sphere determines *how* contentious issues are raised and discussed in public, not necessarily *what* is debated or with what outcome. This observation suggests why civil liberties should not be equated either with political liberties – for example, a democratic suffrage or the rule of parliament – or with a political system *per se*. As components of a political system operating in conjunction with other forces and institutions, civil liberties and the public sphere provide a context and a medium for the expression of public opinion. They do not provide any blueprint of what the ideal state or society might look like.

The 'house divided' viewpoint tends to reduce Wilhelmine politics to a formula. Thus Wehler's 1973 book described the *Kaiserreich* – the term itself is revealing – as a 'semi-absolutist

34

pseudo-constitutional' monarchy. At the same time, Wehler diminished the role of the public sphere to the point that it almost ceased to exist. Pressure groups were 'incorporated into the state' through a kind of 'anti-democratic pluralism'. Inter-party relationships exhibited a 'peculiarly blurred texture'. And although a 'polycratic but uncoordinated authoritarianism' prevailed after 1890, the rival centres of power became 'ossified'. Political forces were contained in an 'inert system' that reduced German liberalism to 'impotence' [291: esp. pp. 64–5].

We have already seen that Wehler's perspective was criticised for its 'top-down' approach. We might also say that it failed to bridge the gap between society-centred and state-centred approaches to the history of politics. One way to reintegrate these approaches is to insert 'political culture' into the equation. We thereby signal that cultural environments, mentalities, and the 'inner meanings' of politics are as important as political systems themselves in determining how society and the state interacted. In Max Kaase's famous quip, trying to define political culture is like trying to nail a pudding to the wall [see Retallack in 148]. Perhaps another image will serve us better. Political culture acts rather like an automobile's transmission, sending forces generated by the motor of social change to the wheels of political decision-making. At the same time it regulates those forces and thereby changes fundamental relationships of power. This is where the conditioning effect of the civil liberties environment and the public sphere becomes important. Diminishing the significance of political culture overemphasises the coherence of strategies for rule worked out by traditional élites or the state: the wheels of change seem to stop and go at the whim of the state, and they steer around any potential shocks to the system.

How, then, is it possible to reassess German political culture before 1918 without going too far in suggesting that the imperial system was modern or could be made so? The appropriate starting point is to consider political institutions and cultural practices that remained largely intact (though not completely unchanged) from 1871 to 1918 [compare overviews in 2; 17: ch. 1; 18: pt. iv; 23; Steinbach in 154; 175: chs 9 and 11].

The empire created in 1871 was unified only to a degree. The constitutional arrangement Bismarck devised was intended to preserve Prussian dominance at the expense of centralised government. Although imperial (Reich) offices were responsible for issues of common national concern, many of these issues were conspicuously uninspiring: commerce, tariffs, transportation, coinage, weights and measures. The federal states – of which the largest were Prussia, Bavaria, Saxony, Baden, and Württemberg – retained administrative and legislative authority over most other issues, including religion, schooling, health, and the exercise of police powers.

During the wars of unification (1864–71) Prussia had provided the force of arms to help bring the German states together, and Prussia constituted roughly two-thirds of Germany's population and territory. So there was no question of this being a union of equals. The head of the federal state was the emperor or Kaiser, who was also king of Prussia. The federal chancellor was the appointed head of the Reich government; with brief and insignificant interruptions he was also minister president in Prussia. Although gradually an imperial bureaucracy was built up, federal legislation was initially drafted in the offices of the Prussian bureaucracy. One reason for this is that Prussia, like the other large states, retained its own state parliament, or Landtag, to which Prussian bureaucrats had been submitting legislation for over twenty years before the founding of the Reich. The Prussian Landtag was based on a system of indirect balloting, and a three-class male suffrage used tax assessments to allot disproportionate political weight to wealthier members of society. As a result, this Landtag, like the Prussian bureaucracy, remained a bastion of conservative interests. Both institutions had such pervasive influence that in the Reich, too, the wheels of state seemed to turn – or more often stop – at the command of Prussian civil servants and Landtag deputies. Yet the other states retained their own assemblies in which the cut-and-thrust of everyday politics was anything but moribund.

What might be referred to as the upper house of the national parliament, the Federal Council (*Bundesrat*), was hardly a sham institution either. Even though it declined in importance over time, it allowed the individual German sovereigns to ensure that the rights of their states were not whittled away. On the other hand, the states' representatives on this council, themselves bureaucrats and generally of a conservative outlook, had little interest in dismantling many of the constitutional powers granted to the Kaiser by the 1871 constitution. Far more important than the Federal Council in giving expression to popular yearnings for democratic rule was the lower house of the imperial parliament, the Reichstag. It consisted of 397 deputies elected on the basis of universal manhood suffrage and an equal, direct, and (theoretically) secret ballot. The Reichstag had the constitutional right to discuss, amend, pass, or reject government legislation. But it was not empowered to draft or initiate legislation itself except in special circumstances. Unlike the British House of Commons, no party or coalition of parties in the Reichstag ever formed the government of the day. The Kaiser alone had the right to appoint and dismiss the chancellor, his state secretaries, and Prussian ministers – all completely independent of the wishes of parliament. Even a majority vote of non-confidence in the chancellor had no formal constitutional implications, and Reichstag deputies did not aspire or expect to be appointed government ministers. The Kaiser also had the final word on foreign policy decisions, and he assumed supreme command of the armed forces in time of war. This, then, was a constitutional monarchy, not a parliamentary democracy. Despite the fact that the universal manhood suffrage for Reichstag elections was more democratic than any other national suffrage in Europe at the time, the constitution ensured that the Kaiser's formal authority in many vital areas of statecraft remained impervious to popular control.

Other elements of Germany's political culture that tended to act as an anchor on reform cannot be encapsulated quite so neatly. Just as some historians lay great emphasis on particular aspects of executive authority – Thomas Nipperdey stresses the Kaiser's supreme military command (*Kommandogewalt*) – others emphasise 'traditionalism' more broadly as a factor tending to undercut all attempts to wrench Germany's political system into the modern era. Examples of such traditionalism have already been mentioned or are considered elsewhere in this study. Geographical and denominational isolation; a persistent attachment to the rhythms of rural life; the influence of religion; the deferential, corporatist mentality of voters in the countryside – these are just some of the factors that prevented full realisation of the liberal, reformist agenda. A related problem is to determine where the 'subject' and the 'citizen' meet, without assuming that the citizen is necessarily less loyal than the subject. This problem colours historians' overall conception of how Germany's political culture evolved after 1890. Anglo-American scholars on balance are inclined to see imperial politics as undergoing fundamental modernisation, whereas German scholars find it more difficult to dismiss the role of tradition. Wherever the balance may lie, Wilhelmine scholarship continues to be enlivened by debates about whether the 'house that Bismarck built' was as shock-proof as it appeared. Fortunately, historians in both camps generally approach such issues as open questions, not as foregone conclusions or as vehicles for dogmatic assertion.

As the exception that proves the rule, a German scholar, Manfred Rauh, proposed a 'silent parliamentarisation' thesis in the 1970s to underscore the reformability of the empire [210; 211]. Rauh catalogued the Reichstag's impressive legislative record and its ability to expand its *de facto* constitutional prerogatives. He also noted the Reichstag's increasingly central place in the popular imagination [see also 73: p. 18]. Rauh stated his thesis too strongly, however. In arguing that anti-parliamentary forces and structures in Prussia had largely been outflanked by 1914, Rauh undervalued the remaining roadblocks to responsible parliamentary government. He also failed to distinguish adequately between parliamentarisation and democratisation. Even the Reichstag's liberal advocates were unwilling to concede that regional and local parliaments should be elected, as the Reichstag was, according to the principal of 'one man, one vote'. Dieter Langewiesche is correct in arguing that the *tension* between 'advancing parliamentarisation and blocked democratisation' is what requires attention [153: p. 641]. Future studies will have to go further, though, to explore how that tension was re-created at the local, state, and national levels of government [e.g. 23; 87; 146; 217; 222; 226: pp. 39–40; 239; 280].

This last point suggests that we are attempting a rather tricky balancing act in asking how Germans confronted the issue of 'repression or reform'. In trying to gauge whether progressive and reactionary forces were becoming more or less polarised over time – in other words, whether confrontation or collaboration was becoming the norm – we must avoid the trap of identifying reforming zeal with the 'people', the parties, or the Reichstag exclusively. Neither these forces nor the state was monolithic. Moreover, not all problems afflicting Wilhelmine political culture were due to the Reich's initial constitutional set-up. Conversely, many constitutional features that had appeared unproblematic in 1871 had become liabilities by 1914. Disaster was hastened both by sidestepping reform and by failing to deal with *new* problems. Therefore any attempt to revise the 'house divided' model must be attentive to nuance and chronological development. Our house of history must indeed have many rooms.

The 'repression or reform' debate came to a head soon after Wilhelm II ascended the throne in 1888. The monarch's confused wish to be a 'people's Kaiser' lay behind the zigzag course in domestic policy. 'The Kaiser is like a balloon', Bismarck remarked before being forced from office: 'If you do not hold fast to the string, you never know where he will be off to' [235: p. 155]. Wilhelm's initial enthusiasm for social reform on behalf of German workers barely lasted the political crisis of early 1890. Thereafter Chancellor Leo von Caprivi's 'new course' (1890–4) tried to foster a less Machiavellian relationship with the liberal parties and national minorities in the Reichstag. By 1893–4, however, Caprivi had exhausted the patience of the conservatives and the Kaiser, who jointly opted for a new dose of repression against the socialists [188; 233; 247; 283; 284]. In 1894 the government introduced an Anti-Revolution Bill in the Reichstag. It failed to pass. Under the government of the aged Chancellor Chlodwig zu Hohenlohe-Schillingsfürst (1894–1900), further measures were introduced to strike at revolutionaries and subversives. In 1895, socialist offices in Berlin were ransacked and party leaders put on trial. In 1899 a law was sent to the Reichstag calling for imprisonment with hard labour for those who threatened strike-breakers. And in 1900 repressive legislation sought to impose stricter censorship against 'immorality' in the press and on the stage [Turk in 51; 143; 157; 283; 284].

Historians still debate the significance of these measures. Most see them in the context of unparalleled political turmoil extending from 1890 to the appointment of Chancellor Bernhard von Bülow in 1900. The historian Karl Lamprecht termed the 1890s an 'age of excitability' (*Zeitalter der Reizsamkeit*) [40: pp. 305–9; also 209]. Lamprecht was alluding to the hypersensitivity of cultural life during this decade, but his observation can apply to the political nervousness of the 1890s as well. Most historians also agree that this decade was imprinted by Wilhelm II – the very embodiment of excitability. Here, too, assessments diverge about what the

Kaiser's 'personal rule' really meant in practice (see Chapters 3 and 4). A third point of consensus is that Bülow's term of office marked a new beginning. It produced an unheralded but significant degree of social reform that contributed to the partial integration of Social Democracy into the Wilhelmine system. Then came a backlash under Chancellor Theobald von Bethmann Hollweg (1909–17), when conservatives argued that social reform had gone far enough.

Where, then, do the main differences of interpretation lie? Two principal camps can be identified. The first includes scholars who emphasise that all of Wilhelm's more repressive schemes were attacked with devastating effectiveness in the political press and defeated on the floor of the Reichstag. Historians interested in the practice of civil liberties and the policing of Wilhelmine society have taken the lead in emphasising the barriers to reaction that were firmly in place by 1900. They have noted that the courts often dismissed frivolous charges, that the rule of law was generally defended – or defended in different ways depending on where one lived – and that local state and municipal authorities frequently refused to grant local police forces the money or authority to implement repression [8; 143; 213; 263; 283]. Moreover, although East German historians were unwilling to concede that the gulf between bourgeois and proletarian society could be bridged, many historians have pointed to increased co-operation between socialists and liberals after 1905 as evidence of political pluralisation. This co-operation was reflected in local and regional parliamentary alliances and in pacts to support each other's candidates at election time [96; 232; 239; 250; 280]. It also facilitated efforts to preserve old barriers to reaction or erect new ones (for example the Reich Association Law of 1908) [Turk and Langewiesche in 117: esp. p. 230; 143: chs 5 and 6]. The publicist Hans Delbrück provided support for this view when he wrote in 1900, referring to the Social Democrats, that 'we have come to the point that we can no longer manage without this party' [275: p. 258].

Historians in the second camp read the historical record very differently. They argue that Wilhelm's frustration with the meagre results of his reactionary agenda in the 1890s actually helped re-establish the 'permanent threat' of a coup d'état (Staatsstreich). In such a coup, martial law would be declared, the army would be unleashed against Reichstag deputies and the Social Democrats in a pre-emptive strike, and the Reichstag suffrage would be revised to gain a more compliant assembly. This option was allegedly a real possibility, partly because the Kaiser and his leading military advisors believed their authority could be shored up in this manner, and partly because the threat achieved its objectives without having to be acted upon [271; 276; 291]. Thus Volker Berghahn has written that the Reichstag was brought into line 'whenever the Kaiser waved a dissolution order' [18: p. 191, also pp. 198, 213, 254–8, 267, 270–1]. Although the rule of law was precariously maintained, reactionary élites successfully convinced the fearful middle classes that socialists were revolutionary, unpatriotic pariahs, 'not worthy to be called Germans'.

In its extreme form, neither of these arguments is entirely acceptable. Although a leftist bloc at one time seemed a vague possibility, this and similar overtures toward responsible government amounted to little before October 1918. On the other hand, those wedded to the concept of a permanent threat of a *coup d'état* have failed to address the most obvious objection of all: that the Kaiser never actually unleashed a decisive strike against his many opponents. Nor for that matter did he ever find a chancellor after Bismarck who was inclined by either temperament or political calculation to consider such a gamble. Even Bülow observed once that 'the German body politic is strong and healthy enough, given time, to eject the Social Democratic poison' [158: p. 84]. To this the proponents of the *coup d'état* thesis reply that the Kaiser never *needed* to embark on a violent course: the Reichstag and the Social Democrats defanged themselves. But why then refer to the *coup d'état* option at all? On balance, an alternative conclusion is more convincing. This recognises that despite their hyperbole, reactionaries possessed neither the strength of will to unleash a civil war at home, nor the backing of public opinion to be certain of victory. The 'threat' was really no threat at all.

The idea that the government repeatedly toyed with the idea of a pre-emptive strike skews our understanding in other ways. Volker Berghahn has drawn a causal link between the Kaiser's inability to unleash a bloodbath against the Social Democrats and the German executive's determination to interpret 'creatively' certain paragraphs of the Criminal Code. To write that 'Justice was blindfolded on just one eye' is suggestive but ultimately misleading.

41

Does this imply that justice could never be impartial? Even more problematic is the assertion that 'ultimately there was always the Army to back up the police saber or the one-eyed Justice' [18: pp. 256–7]. It is one thing to draw attention to particular instances of bureaucratic and legal chicanery. It is quite another thing to suggest that chicanery undermined the rule of law, or that these abuses occurred uniformly throughout the Reich, or that bureaucratic practices were unchanged by the growing force of public opinion. To be sure, questionable legal constructions *were* used from time to time by state prosecutors. Abuses of administrative fairness *did* occur. Certain higher officials *were* predisposed to defend Junker interests. And militarist values *did* permeate German society (see also Chapter 3). Most scholars concede these points. Nevertheless, recent research points in the opposite direction. It sees increasing civil liberties, increasing freedom of the press, and increasing pressure on officials to avoid public scandal by curtailing improper practices [143]. It sees a civil service where diverse patterns of social origin, educational background, and regional service precluded a unified 'ministerial outlook' [29; Witt in 112; 183; Röhl in 258; Witt in 272; 273]. It stresses the remarkable fairness that characterised most election campaigns and balloting procedures [69; 70; 276a: ch. 3]. And it chronicles the army's failure to indoctrinate German youth [95; 162; 246]. The precise weight that should be given to these factors remains in some doubt. But the defenders of the 'people's rights' were clearly more numerous and more powerful than scholars once believed.

Parties and interest groups

We turn now to nutshell descriptions of the major political parties in Wilhelmine Germany, indicating briefly where the revision of older views has been necessary. (For the parties' electoral fortunes, see Figure 2.6.) Actually, historians have directed their main attention in recent years to another task: exploring the relationships *between* these parties and their diverse roles in local and regional political cultures. Those relationships will concern us later in this section.

The two major right-wing parties were the German Conservative Party and the Imperial- and Free Conservative Party. Defending

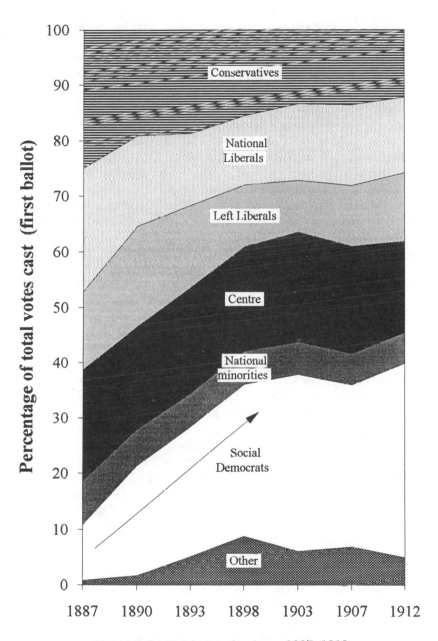

Figure 2.6   Reichstag elections, 1887–1912.
Source: [222: pp. 40–3].

'throne and altar', these parties usually supported government legislation. They drew disproportionate support from Germans with strong monarchist and religious inclinations, including Prussian army officers, higher civil servants, and Protestant pastors. These parties also sought to defend agrarian interests – especially the interests of Prussian Junkers threatened by foreign competition. Both parties suffered decline at the polls. The founding of the Agrarian League (BdL) in 1893 provided the organisational talent and propaganda expertise to offset some of this decline. Hans-Jürgen Puhle's pioneering work in the 1960s argued that although Prussian Junkers called the Agrarian League into existence virtually by an act of will, the anti-Semitic BdL soon 'deformed' German conservatism and Wilhelmine politics as a whole. The 'pre-fascist' Agrarian League set the model for other radical nationalist pressure groups and thereby paved the way for the Nazis. More recently historians have stressed the continued interplay between traditional, reformist, and radical elements within conservatism. They note the marked differences between conservative fortunes in Prussia and in other German states. And they identify their uncertain response to modern politics as the principal reason why conservatives fell between the two stools of *völkisch* radicalism and governmentalism. Puhle's notion of 'pre-fascism' has been one victim of this new viewpoint. Yet historians continue to debate exactly how the old Right and the new Right intersected [39; 53; 54; Stegmann, Eley, and Retallack in 126; 205; 214; 216; 217; 218; Stegmann and Flemming in 272].

The National Liberal Party also generally supported government policy. The same cannot be said of the left liberals, a fractious collection of parties dating back to the 1860s which finally came together in the Progressive People's Party in 1910. Both the National Liberals and the left liberals recruited most of their leaders and members from among Germany's Protestant middle classes, though workers and peasants probably provided the bulk of their voters. These parties supported such policies as further industrial expansion, the defence of civil liberties, and anticlericalism. In many other respects they strayed far from our conception of classical liberalism. The National Liberals, for example, vigorously backed Germany's chauvinistic foreign policy. Even though these parties frequently had to play the nationalist card to keep their supporters united, this tactic did not ensure long-term success. Both older and newer viewpoints stress the susceptibility of the liberal parties to the lures of anti-socialist, anti-democratic, and imperialist slogans even before 1914, prefiguring their inability to meet the Nazi challenge after 1928. Nevertheless, historians have moved away from merely indicting liberal failures. Now they offer a more nuanced exploration of how social, political, and cultural factors undermined popular support for liberal goals. This is helping to reveal new facets of liberalism's role in bourgeois society and its accomplishments in comparison with liberal movements in Britain, France, and elsewhere [25; 87; 117: intro.; 152; 256; still useful for all parties is 189].

The German Centre Party seemed by its name to assign itself to the middle of the political spectrum. Yet because it represented the one-third of Germans who were Catholic, it also deserved its reputation as a 'people's party' (*Volkspartei*), rivalling the achievement of the socialists in establishing an organisational mass base. Also seeking to reflect broad class interests, the Centre tried to be responsive to struggles for social reform and other issues popular among its Catholic constituency. By 1900 it had emerged as the pivotal party in German politics, allying with either right or left as the occasion demanded. Because it did not fit comfortably within the left–right political spectrum, the Centre was seen as a strange interloper. Allegedly having no political weathervane besides a confessional world-view, it was considered by its critics to be cynical, unprincipled, and opportunistic. Recent analyses have tried to work against the grain of contemporary opinion here. They stress that because the Centre responded to the same economic and social pressures that confronted other parties, it was not an exception or an oddity. The Centre's response to democratic reform of the Prussian three-class suffrage, for example, was every bit as ambivalent as that of the liberal parties, not least because sharp differences of opinion divided its regional and national caucuses [21; 22; 33; 146: ch. 9; 163; 164; 241]. It is difficult to predict how far these new perspectives will take us. David Blackbourn has written that in comparing the ambiance of Catholicism with the substance of Centre policies, the medium was decidedly *not* the message. Yet it is still not clear exactly how popular piety actually influenced political practice.

On the extreme left stood the Social Democratic Party (SPD), the pride of the Second International. Like the Centre, the SPD was linked to a distinctive socio-moral milieu – in the SPD's case, to working-class areas mainly (but not exclusively) in Germany's growing cities. Also like the Centre, the SPD was a truly mass-based party – in terms of membership, voters, and organisational structure [93; 221; 229; 244; 254; 278]. By 1912 the SPD and Centre together commanded over 50 per cent of the popular vote and well over half of all Reichstag seats. Yet unlike the Centre, the SPD preserved enough of Marx's theory of socialist revolution to remain beyond the pale as a potential ally to most other parties. Movement here occurred only shortly before the war and without much fanfare. Yet beneath the surface there were forces at work tending to transform the SPD into a modern bureaucratic party. Intellectuals and trade-union leaders diverged in their commitment to revolution, and hierarchical lines of communication began to falter. There was good reason not to be surprised when the SPD's Reichstag deputies voted the funds necessary to wage war in August 1914 and when the mass of German workers rallied to the flag. The relative familiarity of this story has been underlined even as historians have gradually shifted their focus. Now less attention is devoted to the party's intellectual élite, its central organisation, and its confrontation with the state. Instead the social history of the German working classes is recasting debates about the SPD and setting them in a broader socio-economic context (see also Chapter 4) [Breuilly, Crossick, Crew, Lidtke, and Geary are in English in 278; also 79; 160: ch. 1; 228; 229: intro.; 230; 248].

Historians must sometimes choose whether to analyse politics as a system or as a process. The scholarship on smaller Wilhelmine parties and pressure groups illustrates the nature of this choice. Early studies tended to look at the nooks and crannies in the political system into which splinter parties, economic lobbies, and nationalist pressure groups wedged themselves. More recent studies tend to examine the *processes* whereby the parties and interest groups interacted with and transformed each other.

Among the splinter parties were those representing national minorities, anti-Semitic parties, and the more short-lived left-liberal groupings. Among the most important economic lobby groups were the Central Association of German Industrialists and the Agrarian League; the League of German Industrialists and the Hansa League, representing trading interests and light industry; and the local peasants' leagues, including the powerful Bavarian

Peasants' League. Then comes the overwhelming variety of trade unions: the socialist or 'free' trade unions, which attracted the largest memberships, but also the Protestant, Catholic, 'yellow', and unaffiliated unions. Lastly we have to consider a wide range of professional associations, women's organisations, and other advocacy groups [overview in 18: ch. 15]. The organisations that have attracted the most intensive scrutiny of all are the nationalist pressure groups. These include the Pan-German League, the Navy League, the Army League, the Colonial Society, and the Imperial League against Social Democracy [39; 42; 53; 94; 190: ch. 13; Chickering in 197; Puhle in 276]. Virtually all of these organisations, large and small, have been the subject of intensive scholarly work. In the mid-1980s an East German collaborative project published a four-volume handbook that remains the best guide to many of these short-lived or obscure groups [85]. Indeed, it has been said of Friedrich Naumann, founder of the small National Social Association, that he may soon acquire more monographs than he did supporters [256: p. 361]. Yet for English-language readers in particular, there remain huge gaps. We have valuable treatments of National Liberalism in Hessen [298] and Saxony [289], of the Centre Party in Württemberg [21] and the Rhineland [33], of workers in Düsseldorf [193] and Bochum [45]. But considering the vast landscape surrounding these oases, this can be only a beginning. To date there have been surprisingly few works that assess a single party's fortunes throughout the Reich or examine the broad spectrum of parties within a single federal state. Such studies could surely provide an impetus to further synthesis in the way narrower treatments cannot. As Peter Steinbach recently remarked, we should not try to eliminate gaps in our knowledge in the way one might clean a carpet, simply by removing one spot after another until the whole area has been covered [219: p. 72]. In Steinbach's view a more systematic approach is needed to rethink old questions and uncover new ones.

Wilhelmine political culture

The history of political parties is inseparable from the history of elections. In an epoch when most parties did not issue membership cards and when party structures often remained informal,

47

election returns permit us to make our best guesses as to which social groups supported which parties. The late Stanley Suval was a scholar of Wilhelmine elections who suggested that Germans were more uniformly attuned to the positive, 'affirming' act of casting a Reichstag ballot than historians once assumed [276a]. Since Suval's book appeared in 1985, other scholars have studied Reichstag and Landtag elections with increasing intensity and sophistication [69; Fairbairn, Steinbach, and Retallack in 125; 146; 148; 222; 223: sec. iv; Ritter, Steinbach *et al.* in 229; 236; 237; 250]. Taking stock of this recent work, it appears that the notion of the unpolitical German' [Stern in 276] cannot withstand newer evidence about the real (not 'sham') political alternatives confronting Germans both inside and outside the polling booth. Suval demonstrated that the 'right *to* vote' in Reichstag elections was closely connected to the 'rite *of* voting' – that is, a rite that was not just empty ritual. Yet on the state level, a different pattern emerges (*how* different remains open to interpretation). Brett Fairbairn has endorsed Suval's conclusions and demonstrated empirically that Reichstag elections were generally free from overt government manipulation. Yet Thomas Kühne, in studying the very different voting process for Prussian Landtag elections, has shown that Prussia's more complicated balloting procedure actually reinforced traditional habits of deference, especially in the countryside. Debate will continue about the degree to which voting may have affirmed Germans' sense of participating in the system in any given context. But the larger point is that these approaches confirm the logic of viewing Wilhelmine political culture not as an institution but as a process [22; 23]. Another student of German electoral culture provided an even more suggestive metaphor when she wrote that elections provided 'the early handholds, the rough crevices in the smooth system of authority, which allowed some groups of voters . . . to gain a purchase on the wall of *Obrigkeit* [authoritarianism]' [10: p. 1460].

Let us consider two further 'bundles' of strategies devised to illuminate the larger puzzle of Wilhelmine political culture. The first of these, comprising three key concepts, has come to historians by way of political science. Each of these concepts provides a different yardstick to measure what divides political subcultures and what unites them. The second bundle is less concerned with party alignments. It considers instead the broader evolution of political styles. With this approach historians have sought to define a Wilhelmine style of politics, or what Carl Schorske has termed 'politics in a new key'.

1   Turning to the first bundle, the concept of *socio-moral milieu* was developed originally by M. Rainer Lepsius. Lepsius wanted to explain the remarkable degree of continuity in the constellation of German parties and their bases of support, from the mid-nineteenth century well into the twentieth [Lepsius in 139; Ritter in 237]. One aspect of this continuity is evident in Figure 2.6: despite the SPD's growing share of the popular vote, the *lack* of dramatic change in the other parties' fortunes is striking. This relative stability is especially noteworthy in light of mammoth shifts of voter strength in 1928–32, the period of the Nazis' electoral breakthrough. Moreover, most party histories reflect Lepsius's analysis insofar as they identify parties' traditional bastions of support among certain classes, regions, ethnic or confessional groups. The uncommon success of the Centre and SPD in both imperial and Weimar Germany is ascribed to the support they drew from milieux that were culturally more cohesive and nationally more homogenous than the conservative and liberal milieux.

2   The concept of *cleavage* was developed to emphasise divisions that ran between socio-moral milieux or, sometimes, right through the middle of them. The concept of cleavage is most useful in explaining alliances between parties that were based on different milieux but shared common political goals. Four cleavages have been used to explain shifting party coalitions in Wilhelmine Germany: (i) between the centre and the periphery, (ii) between state and church, (iii) between the agrarian and industrial sectors, and (iv) between workers and employers. Yet it has been pointed out that the concept of cleavage fosters a kind of 'sociological determinism'. This concept suggests that groups on either side of a social cleavage – for example, agrarians and industrialists – will always take opposing political positions. But such expectations are often completely wrong [236: pp. 23–4].

3   The concept favoured by Karl Rohe is that of *camps* (*Lager*) [236]. A camp is defined more by what its members oppose than by what unites them. Therefore a camp can be much more heteroge-

49

neous than a milieu. It can even bring together groups divided by cleavages. Thus agrarians and industrialists can work together to hold the socialists at bay. Yet a camp is more than just a convenient or momentary coalition. It is built on powerful historical, cultural, and emotional foundations. These foundations make it rather easy to transfer one's allegiance from one party to another *within* the camp. But they make it very difficult to move *between* camps.

Each of these concepts speaks to larger questions about German political development. Some historians argue that the inability of German parties to break out of the mould established in the mid-nineteenth century largely explains their failure in the face of the Nazi threat. Another view holds that dramatic shifts within the nationalist camp after 1928 – to the almost exclusive advantage of the Nazis – are partly explained by the inability of *Wilhelmine* Germans to cross the great divide that separated the socialist and nationalist camps. Consensus remains elusive. On the one side remain those who favour the polarisation view. These historians suggest that Wilhelmine politics by 1914 had become so divided into opposing blocs that it had reached a 'stalemate', a 'dead end', a 'latent crisis', or a 'blind alley' [*inter alia*, 175: ch. 11; 192: vol. 2, pp. 574–6; Ritter intro. and Schmidt in 226; 251; Schmidt and Puhle in 276]. On the other side are those who stress the opportunities for movement or who believe, contrary to the *Sonderweg* thesis, that German political development was not uniquely burdened by party structures and practices dating from the mid-nineteenth century [e.g. 148]. There is no definitive way to reconcile these viewpoints at present, or even to judge their heuristic value precisely. The fractured nature of German nationalism, for instance, immediately calls into doubt the idea of a 'nationalist camp'.

What of the second bundle of approaches – those put forward by historians who feel that not political *alignments* but political *styles* changed most dramatically in the 1890s? These historians work from the premise that the deferential 'politics of notables' (*Honoratiorenpolitik*) characteristic of the Bismarckian age was left behind under the impact of rapid political mobilisation of the masses. As a result, 'professional patriots' and other rabble-rousers came to the fore, seeking to portray themselves as outsiders but also as tribunes of the people (hence the label 'populists'). These men – and a few women – denounced the élitist practices of estab-

50

lished parties and argued that the age of universal suffrage necessitated the expansion of the political nation [22: chs 6, 8, and 10;
39; 41; 53; 126; 214]. Sometimes they worked within the system,
sometimes they promised to dismantle it entirely. Some embraced
extreme racist views and made it their life's work to defend Germany from a 'flood' of Slavs or Jews. Others voiced the real
economic woes of the lower-middle classes.

Debate has arisen as to whether these figures were actually outsiders at all or whether they were drawn from the same social
circles as the traditional party élites. Geoff Eley has argued that
radical nationalists were drawn mainly from the lower-middle
classes. Roger Chickering, with his cultural study of the Pan-
German League, has located radical nationalism firmly within the
upper-middle-class milieu – that is, among the ranks of the educated bourgeoisie who were no strangers to politics. This debate
cannot be reduced to a kind of 'self-mobilisation from below'
versus 'manipulation from above' polarity. David Blackbourn,
examining what he calls the 'spiral of demagoguery' leading to the
Third Reich, has chosen instead the idea of a volatile 'push–pull'
relationship between older élites and discontented social groups.
What unites Blackbourn, Eley, and Chickering is their view that
nationalism did not remain identified exclusively with the interests
of the German state. Nationalism, far from being a tool of the
government to rally support, became a weapon for challenging the
legitimacy of the state and for proposing more extreme nationalist
alternatives. (One such alternative was proposed by the Pan-
German leader Heinrich Claß in his book, *If I Were Kaiser*, published anonymously in 1912.) What one historian terms the 'verbal
shot-gun scatter of resentment' and what another describes as the
struggle for control of Germany's national symbols represent two
sides of the same coin. By 1914 nationalist appeals to the will of
the people had taken on an ominous tone.

Less convincing is the practice of singling out the 1890s as the
'crucial watershed' in the rise of mass politics [e.g. Eley in 117;
Eley and Stegmann in 126; compare 10: p. 1471; 216; Steinbach in
229: p. 6]. Something changed after 1890, or at least appeared to
change. That much is clear. The psychological impact of Bismarck's departure from office can as little be ignored as the
political effect of the lapsing of the anti-socialist law and the rapid
growth of the SPD. But were the early 1890s a 'populist moment'

in history, an 'absolutely crucial turning point'? Any view that isolates this decade neglects many decisive breakthroughs before 1890. Of these, the German people's painful accommodation to the universal Reichstag suffrage after 1867 is the most significant. A view focused on the 1890s can also misrepresent political innovations that became important only after 1900. Looking at municipal politics, one finds that what contemporaries defined as 'hateful politicking' did not appreciably change the tenor of local politics until after the turn of the century [Pogge in 125; 257; 273: ch. 7]. Moreover, the emergence of a decisively radical, 'modern' brand of anti-Semitism arguably occurred *not* in the 1890s but rather – paradoxically – both before and after: first in the late 1870s (some would say even earlier), and then again in the final years of the war [206; 286]. In fact anti-Semitism has been strangely downplayed in most studies of radical nationalism.

Many of these issues can be addressed with a more careful definition of terms. What precisely was 'new' about politics in a new key? What role did the 'masses' play in mass politics? How 'radical' was radical nationalism? Who exactly were the 'demagogues' and 'demigods' who anticipated Hitler? What did it mean when political activists spoke of 'demagoguery in the good sense'? The style of politics after 1900 was light years away from what it had been under Bismarck. But it was also worlds apart from the style of the Nazis. Compared to the typical Nazi rally, even the discussion evenings staged by the radical Pan-German League remained remarkably patrician and stuffy. 'Terrible, terrible!', was Hitler's reaction in *Mein Kampf* when he recalled the narrow patriotism and 'cultivation of sociability' that still characterised German nationalism in the late Wilhelmine era [see 39: epilogue; Chickering and Bessel in 125: esp. p. 311]. Perhaps, then, this was actually still politics in the *old* key.

In the end it remains difficult to find a good fit among all the components of the Wilhelmine political system. But this is because we now have a richer understanding of the plurality of forces at work. Whereas earlier accounts of Wilhelmine politics were characterised by an overly mechanical account of how parties and interest groups functioned, we now consider systemic tensions and popular passions together. These defined the larger cultural worlds of politics, albeit in ways that most Germans before 1918 only dimly understood.

Education, Minorities, and Gender Relations

The concept of political culture is only one means to explore link-ages between the worlds of politics and culture. Individuals are trained in social behaviour no less than in political behaviour by cultural contexts and practices. Each stage of personal develop-ment may offer different lessons, but many influential factors are fixed for life. This section examines some of these factors – geo-graphic origin, religious denomination, ethnicity, gender – as a means to explore relationships between culture and power as con-cretely as possible. Our principal aim cannot be to determine how intersecting cultural worlds determined specific political outlooks, for in most cases no definitive conclusion can be drawn. This point is conceded even by historians who stress the unfortunate effects of German patterns of socialisation. For example, Wehler dismissed the tendency to equate patriarchal relations within the German family with a predisposition to authoritarianism or fas-cism: 'The New England Puritan, the Victorian Englishman and the Republican Frenchman', wrote Wehler, 'were scarcely outdone in terms of severity by the Wilhelmine father-figure' [291: p. 119]. A more useful approach is to consider to what extent contempo raries were aware of an interplay between external forces operating upon them and internalised forces *within* them. This approach in turn provides more clues as to why German responses to modernity were so ambivalent.

Shulamit Volkov has suggested in this context that anti-Semitism was an important 'cultural code' because it provided a means for Germans to sum up their distaste for quite unrelated features of modern life [286: ch. 1]. This 'code' provided a common language for Germans wishing to situate themselves within the dominant culture. The concept of 'cultural codes' can be useful in examining other processes of socialisation, too, especially when we wish to consider the roles of tradition and convention in setting limits – *cultural* limits, not just political limits – to reform. In the longest chapter of his *German Empire* book, Wehler examined how such conventions helped bind together the 'matrix of authoritarian so-ciety'. By determining how the individual was 'enmeshed' in society, these conventions contributed to the 'regulation of conflict', the 'ideology of legitimation', and the 'subservient men-tality' so characteristic of Wilhelmine society [291: esp. p. 118].

Many scholars now doubt whether the typical German was shaped by cultural conventions in the deterministic manner postulated by Wehler. Yet few would deny a fundamental linkage between two of Wehler's most immediate concerns: cultural devices tending toward the integration of German society, and structural hostility toward liberal democracy.

Schools, universities, and the enrolment explosion

Schools allocate social opportunity. Although some features of the Wilhelmine education system mirrored the rigid class nature of German society, others reflected and reinforced social change. In primary education, expansion and differentiation were necessary to meet the demands of a literate, mobile, industrial society. This helps explain why the *Volksschule*, the 'school of the masses', was the battleground on which the Kaiser, the political parties, and the churches fought for the minds of Germany's youth. Inaugurating a decade of intense debate over school reform, Wilhelm II issued a decree in May 1889 that left no doubt about the importance of schooling in inculcating social discipline: 'In an age when Social Democratic heresies and distortions are communicated with increasing energy, the schools must make a greater effort to teach what is truthful, what is real, and what is possible in the world' [154: p. 159]. What we know about the rigid discipline dispensed during primary school lessons suggests that teachers took the Kaiser's admonition to heart. Yet *Volksschule* curricula became at the same time more national and more modern. Language instruction emphasised High German over local dialects; but it included a new technical vocabulary. History lessons stressed the accomplishments of the empire over those of particularist dynasties; but enthusiasm for Prussia did not penetrate to all corners of the Reich [134; 150; 192: vol. 1, pp. 538–9; 195; Kelly in 197].

The traditional German grammar school, the *Gymnasium*, offered middle-class youths aged 10–18 a classical humanist education. Previously the *Gymnasium* alone granted the school-leaving certificate (*Abitur*) necessary to enter university and to serve as a 'one-year volunteer' in the army. But reformist pedagogues and the bourgeoisie advocated opening the system up, modernising it, and making it more accessible to girls [6; 7]. Hence

54

the newer *Realgymnasien* and the *Oberrealschulen* expanded at a tremendous rate. Between 1882 and 1911, the number of Prussian students attending *Realgymnasien* increased by about 80 per cent (from about 27,000 to over 48,000). The even more popular *Oberrealschulen* increased their attendance some ten-fold [192: vol. 1, p. 555; 275: p. 139]. Together these schools attracted mainly bourgeois students who were happy to spend fewer hours on the obligatory lessons in Latin and Greek that still tormented students in the élite schools. Figure 2.7 contrasts the differing curricula available.

Between 1890 and 1914, total German university enrolments increased from about 28,000 to about 60,000 students. According to one scholar, this increase represented the 'transition from the traditional élite to a modern middle-class university' [114: p. 156]. Largely unplanned and unregulated, this expansion led to worries about an 'overabundance' of university-trained graduates. Yet it was necessary to give greater recognition to the technical universities (*Technisiche Hochschulen*) which offered more up-to-date curricula. This development hardly solved the problem of access. Large segments of the population remained disadvantaged. Catholics were underrepresented because they came disproportionately from rural areas [22: ch. 9; Ross in 51]. Women were allowed to sit in on university lectures beginning in the mid-1890s, but they could not enrol for courses leading to graduation until Easter 1909. By 1914 over 4000 women were enrolled in German universities [7; 192: vol. 1, p. 578]. Most disadvantaged and underrepresented of all were workers. Nevertheless, as noble self-recruitment fell off, a university degree came within the grasp of the lower-middle classes: white-collar workers, shopkeepers, less affluent businessmen, the poorer clergy, and private teachers. Among university faculties, too, broader recruitment of personnel and structural diversification emphasised the plurality of the system. Although the magnitude of these changes may seem modest by today's standard, in the view of many contemporaries the 'mass university' and the 'multiversity' were both born in the Wilhelmine age.

Moving from social contexts to political consequences, one finds less consensus among historians. Some explain the amalgamation of the old and new educated élites as evidence that the Wilhelmine bourgeoisie was co-opted into the political estab-

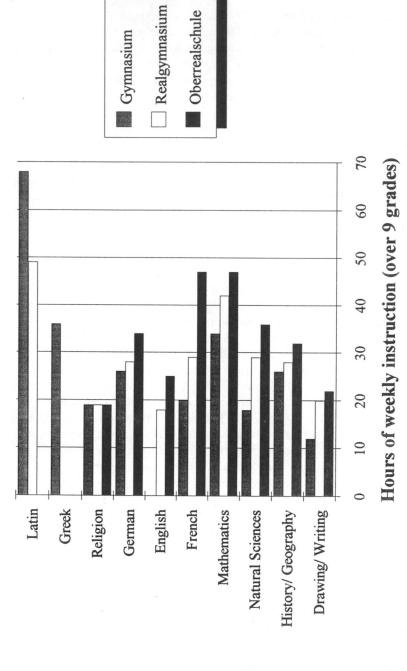

Figure 2.7 Secondary school curricula in Prussia, 1901.
Source: [192: vol. 1, p. 553].

lishment. Studying 'academic illiberalism' within the student subculture, Konrad Jarausch has identified an extreme anti-Semitic, nationalist, and imperialist strain within it. Jarausch and others have also described the professoriat's withdrawal into the world of 'objective' scholarship and its enthusiasm for war in 1914 [inter alia, vom Bruch in 50; 114; 177: ch. 9,]. Other historians paint a brighter picture [e.g. McClelland and Jarausch in 51; 167; 191: ch. 8]. They emphasise that German universities were more accessible than those in England and France; that prominent critics of the Wilhelmine establishment used their professorial chairs as vital outposts in the public sphere; and that Germans were unequalled in their pioneering research – measured, for instance, by the number of Nobel Prizes won in the sciences.

On balance, despite much evidence about pedagogical chauvinism, it would be wrong to stress the authoritarian aspects of German higher education too strongly. German universities *were* envied and copied by reformers around the world. One American admirer called them 'a jewel in the imperial crown' [51: p. 169]. Traditional political views could not withstand the onslaught of modernisation. Because the German educational system underwent such a fundamental transformation, by 1914 even conservatives within its ranks could not hope to fulfil the goals Wilhelm had outlined in 1889.

Religious and national minorities and their subcultures

Living with the legacy of the Holocaust and confronting the horror of 'ethnic cleansing' in south-east Europe, we can perhaps comprehend something of the power of racial and ethnic prejudice in Wilhelmine Germany. From our largely secularised age – notwithstanding the headlines still grabbed by papal encyclicals, Islamic fundamentalism, and Christian revivalism – it is much more difficult to understand the subtle impact of religion before 1918. Yet religion was one of the most important cleavages running through Wilhelmine society. In rural and small-town life especially, the church was – and was *seen* to be – firmly on the side of authority. Whether one was a Protestant, a Catholic, a Jew, or a member of a dissenting faith, to stand outside the religious establishment altogether was to be decidedly abnormal. Usually such a

57

stance required great personal courage or an alternative belief system such as Marxism [21; 27; Mallmann and Blessing in 164; Schieder in 249; 261].

It may be true that early research on religion in nineteenth-century Germany more often asserted than demonstrated 'the authoritarian hold of Lutheran [or Catholic] ideology at a popular level' [291: p. 114]. This seems to be changing. The long-standing sensitivity to the importance of religion found in the work of Thomas Nipperdey and Wolfgang Schieder has won many converts of late, substantiating Nipperdey's claim that 'confessional division and tension was one of the fundamental, vital facts of everyday life in Germany'. Helmut Walser Smith's *German Nationalism and Religious Conflict* (1995), for example, has examined both religious affinities and antagonisms to suggest why 'cultural divisions between regions, nationalities, and religious groups often influenced daily life as much as, and sometimes more than, class inequality' [261: pp. 6, 13].

We have already discussed developments in the history of political Catholicism. Despite the pivotal position of the Centre Party, the Catholic minority suffered many disadvantages that contributed to its persistent isolation. Some of these were based on hard-nosed political calculation by the Centre's opponents. National Liberals in positions of influence were notorious for denigrating Catholicism as incompatible with learning and gress. This attitude was enough to create a climate of discrimination in many regions. Other systemic roadblocks also stood in the path to success: Catholicism's relatively rural character on the periphery of the Reich (in Silesia, Poznan, Bavaria, Baden, and the Rhineland); antagonistic relations between ethnic groups in these areas; and woefully inadequate educational opportunities. Thus the Catholic population was indeed underrepresented among the pool of applicants for civil service jobs and academic appointments. It also provided few success stories within Germany's expanding entrepreneurial élite [22: ch. 9; Ross in 51; Mooser and Schloßmacher in 164]. Catholics often perceived discrimination against them by the state, where in reality it was these systemic factors that precluded a satisfactory resolution of the so-called 'parity issue'.

Discrimination against national minorities is another issue of obvious relevance to the historical debate about socio-political

58

pluralisation or polarisation [overviews in 18: pp. 110-23; Kleßmann in 154; 204: pp. 28-32; see also 192: vol. 2, pp. 266-86]. There is little doubt that the incorporation of significant national minorities at the birth of the Reich fed the fantasies of those who believed that Germany had a national mission to Germanise Central Europe. For these hyper-nationalists, religious and ethnic minorities within German borders constituted a direct threat to the new nation. The Polish minority alone constituted some 5.5 per cent of the total population of Germany. In Prussia, one in eleven citizens spoke Polish. Although the French population in Lorraine and the Danish population in Schleswig were much smaller, together with the Poles they numbered over 4 million.

One can hardly overemphasise the range of experiences among these groups, reflecting the diverse ways in which discrimination was exercised. German language policy in Alsace-Lorraine was relatively flexible and tolerant, despite occasional flare-ups [252; 292: ch. 2]. The Protestant Masurians and Lithuanians also suffered little overt discrimination, while the Guelphs organised a regional political party to fight for the privileges of the deposed Hanoverian dynasty. The light touch of German federalism was never apparent in Prussia's Polish policy, however. Chancellor Bülow's language legislation after 1900 gave rise to a political crisis of national proportions: a mass strike by over 40,000 Polish schoolchildren in 1906 [94; 144; 292: ch. 7]. Together with the Prussians' equally ill-fated settlement policy in Poznan and west Prussia, this repression fuelled rather than dampened Polish nationalism. The experience of Polish workers in the Ruhr has drawn new attention to national subcultures. Historians still disagree as to whether working-class Poles integrated themselves into the 'melting pot' of Ruhr life, or whether they even wished to do so [Bade and Kleßmann in 14; 54: ch. 8; 145; 184; 292: ch. 9]. But scholars are aware that a more nuanced consideration of these questions must address a broader range of socialising influences, including regional political cultures, associational networks, the church, popular piety, the press, and social habits ingrained in neighbourhood life [e.g. 231: pp. 427-8].

Whereas most Poles were industrial or agricultural labourers, most German Jews were solidly middle class. This invariably coloured perceptions of the 'Jewish problem' [159; 181; 190: ch. 6; 206; 207; 243; 286]. On the one hand, many lower- and upper-class

59

Germans associated Jews with what they condemned about middle-class liberalism specifically or bourgeois culture generally: unimpeded individualism, the profit motive, the preferment of the professions over 'productive' labour, or the lack of ethical standards in the press and on the stage. On the other hand, the non-Jewish bourgeoisie itself was growing more defensive on questions of race and national identity. This sensitivity widened the gulf between middle-class Gentiles and middle-class Jews: the anti-Semitic parties soon realised that the largest reservoir of potential recruits lay among these middle strata.

Objectively, the proportion of Jews in the German population was shrinking: from 1.25 per cent in 1871 to under 1 per cent in 1910 (or about 615,000 persons). However, to contemporaries it appeared that pressures for Jewish assimilation – demonstrated, for example, by the rising number of mixed marriages – were not having the desired effect. The same seemed to be true of official discrimination against Jews [207: chs 2 and 3.5]. Neither force was strong enough to weaken the 'enemy within'; neither diverted the 'golden international' from its alleged goal to conquer the German nation. Even Christian tolerance broke down as conservatives from both the Catholic and Protestant faiths tended to view Judaism as the point of the liberal dagger aimed at the heart of German culture [22: ch. 8; Blaschke in 164]. As one anti-Semitic professor wrote: 'Liberalism, Judaism, Mammonism, Socialism, Pessimism, Anarchism, Nihilism – that is the ladder down which we are climbing . . . into the abyss' [88: p. 161; 277]. Against these arguments Jewish attempts at self-defence seemed hesitant and unconvincing [149]. Even those Jews who offered a more positive message, whether through preservation of a distinctive Jewish culture or through Zionism, found that they alienated former liberal defenders, who had hoped that the Jewish question would disappear once full assimilation was accomplished.

To understand these disappointments one must avoid equating assimilation and integration. In light of present-day examples of multicultural societies, there is no overriding reason why German society could not have integrated a minority that turned away from a strictly assimilationist position. Recent historians of German Jewry suggest that assimilation – that is, submersion in the dominant culture – is not necessarily the normative path in societies where ethnic or religious groups live side by side [18: p. 96]. Instead, 'acculturation' is a more useful analytical term, allowing historians to discard notions of Jewish self-hatred that emphasise Jews' false consciousness. Instead of concentrating on Jews' failure to assimilate, historians are now turning to the study of a Jewish subculture where the affirmation of Jewish identity was anything but incompatible with economic success and social acceptance [13; van Rahden in 27; Volkov in 141; 286: chs 6 and 7]. To take just one example of such work, Marion Kaplan has demonstrated how Jewish housewives kept Jewish culture alive in the home, even while assisting their husbands gain recognition outside it [130]. This perspective sometimes disregards the pervasive influence of political anti-Semitism on social relations and cultural values. Yet there is value in suggesting that the later course of German–Jewish relations was hardly on the horizon in 1914. As Peter Gay has written:

For German Jews anxious to live and work in peace, as Germans, the persistence of [anti-Semitic] . . . centers of darkness and animosity still scattered across the social landscape seemed so unpleasant precisely because so much had happened in the way of liberalization and enlightenment. But the main point was that much *had* happened. [88: p. 93]

Gender and sexuality

'Years went by without my noticing that I was young', wrote the later socialist Ottilie Baader in her autobiography. 'Sitting year after year at the sewing machine, always the collars and cuffs before me, one dozen after another; there was no value to life. . . . I saw and heard nothing of all the beautiful things in the world; I was simply excluded from all that' [133: pp. 72–3]. That Karin Hausen could give a recent essay the subtitle 'The Social History of the Sewing Machine' illustrates the new appreciation of gender as an analytical category to discuss German industrialisation and changes in German society [Hausen in 112; Maynes in 57]. As research on working-class women has taken off since the late 1970s and 1980s, the gendered dimension of socio-economic change has come into sharper focus [e.g. 82; 83]. Yet early work on German women also concentrated on reprinting autobiographies, examining how the German feminist movement was splintered by divergent aims and methods, and documenting this movement's notable lack of success in winning the extension of political liberties (especially the vote) to women [59; 61; 81]. Often a great divide appeared in this literature between middle-class and proletarian experiences, and a comparative perspective was often neglected to the point that the German experience of gender conflict remained largely unrelated to the experiences of modernising societies elsewhere. Still, this work gradually demonstrated the range of women's protests against legal, educational, and political discrimination. It revealed, for instance, that the new German Civil Code of 1900 actually diminished certain rights for women.

More recent research has tended to concentrate on the mentalities that conditioned women's responses to everyday problems [Canning and Quataert in 57; Rosenhaft in 125]. For example, we now have a better window on working-class women's response to definitions of skill based on gender. Why, after all, should we assume that male workers first became class conscious on the shop-floor but that women's identities were shaped in the realm of home and family [e.g. Schulte in 68; Canning in 125]? We now also see more clearly how bourgeois women strained to reconcile their 'manly' duties as household managers, their 'pedagogical' duties as mothers, and their 'passive' duties as wives (both in and outside the conjugal bed) [83: chs 10 and 11; 84]. Of course not every monograph can cover such broad social terrain. While one might 'usher us in through the front portal, take us round the [rooms for entertaining visitors] and finally lead us into the family quarters and the marital bedroom', another 'slips us in quietly through the servants' entrance and shows us a slice of life below stairs' [65: p. 629].

As research has become more sophisticated, we have come to understand the many subtle ways in which conflicting cultural codes contributed to German anxieties about gender roles. Working-class mothers, for example, bore the double burden of work and family; but many of their husbands or partners also suffered a 'role strain' in having to rely on a second family income. Similarly, middle-class wives were responsible for what Sibylle Meyer has termed 'the tiresome work of conspicuous leisure' [169]; but their husbands rarely acknowledged the tensions inherent in maintaining the charade that their wives led satisfying lives of idleness and plenty.

Recent studies of masculinity have laid bare other anxieties that had their genesis in the dictates of social convention. Interestingly, many of these studies demonstrate a point made earlier: that few epochs in history have been more closely scrutinised than the Wilhelmine period for evidence of pathological trends leading to later disasters. Three examples of this approach can be cited: (i) a study of 'male fantasies' which examines the experience of Wilhelmine youths who contributed to the cult of masculinity in Free Corps units after 1918 [279: esp. vol. 2, pp. 350–1]; (ii) studies of duelling which reach different conclusions about whether the German duel was uniquely male-oriented, uniquely bourgeois, or even uniquely German [Frevert in 25; Frevert in 141; 166]; and (iii) a study of a pro-fascist political philosopher of the 1920s and 1930s, Carl Schmitt, whose early writings attacked Wilhelmine homosexuality in order to undermine liberal-democratic ideals [262]. Although none of these works is concerned *exclusively* with the Wilhelmine period, each of them identifies an intensive rethinking of traditional gender roles in the pre-1918 era that had large implications for later developments.

Ute Frevert has noted that any society putting strong emphasis on self-discipline and mastery over one's emotions will naturally also 'seek to regulate human sexuality and harness it to other social norms' [83: p. 131]. This observation prompts the question of just how up-tight or hypocritical Germans actually were, compared to, say, their better-studied counterparts in Victorian England. Many factors conspired against any attempt to overcome such sexual taboos in Wilhelmine Germany as premarital and extramarital sex. Those taboos in turn made it difficult to acknowledge that not only 'bawdy' women might enjoy sex. Two final examples illustrate that current approaches to questions of gender and sexuality in Wilhelmine Germany reveal the consequences of attempts to preserve 'separate spheres' for men and women. John Fout has examined the homosexual rights movement as well as the moral purity leagues which launched a 'sustained, vicious, and politically effective counterattack' against it [80]. Why this viciousness? Convictions for male homosexuality showed only a modest rise during the Wilhelmine era, and Berlin police tolerated about forty homosexual bars and 1000–2000 male prostitutes in 1914 [52a: p. 83]. Fout's answer is twofold. First, the moral purity movement only ostensibly targeted male homosexuals; it really took aim at feminists, critics of the church, and undisciplined youth. Second, the battle over vice was really a struggle to maintain traditional gender roles: 'If homosexuality had not existed', writes Fout, 'the [moral purity] movement would have had to invent [it]' [80: p. 420; also 270].

Whereas the moral purists side-tracked an open discussion of sexuality, new ideas could more successfully be advanced by wrapping them in the scientific vocabulary of eugenics [9]. The eugenics movement was determined to practice 'racial hygiene' in order to preserve 'the future of the nation'. Its success illustrated how broadly Social Darwinist ideas were diffused in German society. One can again ask how much the Germans differed from other Europeans in stressing collective over individual responsibility. One might also note that public discussion of this issue was carried on mainly by men. Yet to stress either point too vehemently would go against the grain of recent scholarship, which avoids overdrawing a picture of women's suffering, marginality, and self-contempt [e.g. 5; Franzoi in 81]. Women used hidden, 'subversive' strategies of empowerment to expand the limits of the separate sphere accorded them in both public and private life. Thus even female eugenicists cannot be dismissed simply as willing victims to patriarchal fashions and conservative politics. Instead they helped establish a new agenda by seeking to drive Germany's 'national destiny' forward, not backward. In piecing together a composite picture of recent research, then, one is struck by the characteristically modern features of the Wilhelmine debate about the 'woman's predicament', traditional gender roles, and human sexuality. For women and men alike, though not in equal measure and not in the same ways, the Wilhelmine era brought the Janus face of modernisation into view for the first time.

Culture and the 'Wilhelmine Mood'

The birth of the modern

'In all Germany', wrote the historian Friedrich Meinecke, 'one can detect something new around 1890, not only politically, but also spiritually and intellectually' [8: p. 222]. Developments in science and scholarship offer a starting point to explore the new tone in Wilhelmine culture. The German intellectual community brought into close contact scientists, artists, and other thinkers who refused to conceive of their calling narrowly. Gradually the word 'culture' was infused with more inflated significance than categorical preci-sion. Here the universities contributed to 'the cult of *Technik*' – the 'emphasis on scientism, efficiency, and management' on the one hand, and the reflection of 'an awareness of weakness and diffu-sion' on the other [52a: p. 70; also 111; 177; 287]. The sudden medical interest after 1890 in neurasthenia as a reflection of the 'nervous' times is another illustration of the same cultural syn-drome [209]. Even as the real world was demystified in rational terms, its deeper human mysteries were probed for the first time.

Far more than in the age of Bismarck, scientific scholarship was called upon to answer critically important questions about techni-cal and social progress. Yet society's thirst for 'total' answers could not be quenched. In the new field of theoretical physics, Max Planck's quantum theory (1900) and Albert Einstein's special theory of relativity (1905) undermined notions of continua and absolutes. Atomic chemists were turning to questions of stability and decay, and geneticists were exploring mutation theory and the inconstancy of genetic material. Among the humanities and social sciences, historicism stressed that the lessons of the past provide no social, moral, and political truths for all time, while psychology and anthropology drew attention to the importance of intuition, myth, appearance, and primitivism. Sociologists such as Georg Simmel, Ferdinand Tönnies, and Max Weber saw the complexity of such 'provocative' phenomena as huge cities, modern bureauc-racies, and mass politics [174]. The philosopher Friedrich Nietzsche proclaimed that 'God is dead' because, for him, the idea of a traditional God presupposed the same absolute truths for religion and society that Newtonian physics had postulated for the universe. After the turn of the century Nietzsche's teachings achieved immense popularity: such aphorisms as 'become what you are' (rather than what you 'should' be) caught the imagination of a bourgeois German public anxious about the future. Yet Nietzsche's fascination with anti-bourgeois, messianic, and hyper-idealistic themes also mirrored views found in Germany's academic community [Waite in 187].

65

Although the Wilhelmine state took its role as a patron of German culture seriously, new social, political, and artistic pressures changed the ties that linked artists and their public. This was an age when the bourgeoisie had more money, time, and interest to invest in highbrow culture. Certainly Wilhelm and his appointees attempted to impose limits on what art would be produced and what message it would convey. In a speech in December 1901, Wilhelm demonstrated his understanding that art could be politically subversive. 'When art,' he declared, 'shows us only misery, as often happens today, . . . then art commits a sin against the German people. . . . [Art must] hold out its hand to raise the people up, instead of descending into the gutter' [198: p. 25]. Yet here, as in so many things, Wilhelm achieved the exact opposite of what he intended. By handing down such pronouncements from on high, he only increased the determination of artists to seek new styles and techniques. Wilhelm thereby promoted exactly the sort of art he most disliked. In 1898 the Kaiser vetoed a medal that was to have been awarded to Käthe Kollwitz for her graphic cycle, *The Weavers*. Wilhelm believed that Kollwitz's art – like Gerhard Hauptmann's drama of the same name – sought to inflame class hatred. 'But from then on,' Kollwitz later recalled, 'at one stroke, I was counted among the foremost artists of the country' [37: p. 468]. Developments in architecture displayed the same unintended dialectical effect. In his 1901 speech Wilhelm declared that 'the magnificent remnants of classical antiquity' revealed 'an eternal, unchanging law . . . the law of aesthetics' [198: p. 25]. But after 1890, architects, designers, and city planners would no longer put up with the Olympian motifs and blustering façades of previous eras; they moved on to simpler, less cluttered forms [Trommler in 57].

Of course artists have always resisted orthodoxy and social convention. We should not imagine that even a majority of Wilhelmine artists turned their backs completely on the establishment. Most simply could not afford to [Deschmukh in 37; 47; 185; 198]. Nevertheless, the official monopoly on galleries, exhibits, and sources of funding declined after 1890. This development fuelled a pluralisation of popular tastes and a democratisation of the market. The ascendancy of a single artist or conception of culture – Richard Wagner and 'Wagnerism', for example – is inconceivable for the period after 1890. This plurality contributed to the success of German artists in helping to realise at least part of the Modernist agenda, seeking new forms of symbol, metaphor, and myth through Post-Impressionism and Expressionism. Yet artists also grew more self-critical and divided. Some sought beauty and a higher truth. Others displayed a fascination with violence, decadence, illness, and death; to shock an audience, a touch of the bizarre or grotesque might be added. That Germany had many cultural centres – most notably Berlin, Dresden, and Munich – gave each secession from the cultural mainstream a different flavour [118].

What, if anything, united German artists as *Germans*? The campaign to build national monuments after 1890 revealed that artists shared the public's anxiety about the beleaguered nature of the empire. Thus their new identity was prone to misinterpretation at home and abroad (Nietzsche had understood this in the 1870s). Having embraced themes of the apocalypse, it was impossible for most German artists and intellectuals to withstand the lure of war in August 1914. Having sought to wed primitive and ultramodern styles in art, German intellectuals did not know which way to face when their own conception of national culture came under fire. Their reactions illustrated Erwin Panofsky's later observation that art, and the study of art, are both part of 'man's proud and tragic consciousness' [200: p. 710; also 47; vom Bruch in 50; 177: pt 2; 199].

Popular culture

From 1945 to the late 1960s, studies of intellectual life in imperial Germany tended to search for early strains of Nazi ideology. In this enterprise, scholars such as Ralf Dahrendorf, George Mosse, and Fritz Stern opened many doors [274]. Critics of this approach soon argued that excavating history in this manner reads intellectual developments backward exclusively from the perspective of the Nazi era and the Holocaust. In the 1970s this critique produced a partial turning-away from intellectual history. Not all historians agreed that the role of ideology should be downplayed or marginalised, however. In the 1980s the 'new cultural history' began to show that this marginalisation diminished our understanding of Wilhelmine culture in the broad sense. When cultural history concerns itself with the values and mentalities of modernising societies, when it seeks to explore deeper issues of power and identity, it can contribute to a rethinking of accepted truths about social, economic, and political change as well.

New approaches have nourished scholarship on Wilhelmine popular culture particularly. Popular culture cannot be wholly identified with mass entertainment, and still less with working-class entertainment. These aspects of popular culture were none the less excluded from historical discussion for many years by the SPD's attempts to ensure that German workers were offered only reading matter and cultural pursuits that were morally edifying and politically didactic [Trommler in 187]. This exclusionary premise contributed to the relative neglect of popular culture by East German historians, though with a few notable exceptions [49; 182].

Popular culture took on a new character around the turn of the century due to higher disposable incomes, shorter working hours, and the emergence of a distinctive urban lifestyle attuned to the desires of German youth. Just as important was the proliferation of new *forms* of entertainment and leisure activities. Traditional amusements passed down from early-modern times did not die out overnight: parish fairs and neighbourhood pubs still figured prominently among working-class leisure pursuits. After 1900, however, entrepreneurial initiative began to take over. Technological progress and market forces soon drove an identifiably modern entertainment industry. Cabarets, cinemas, and dance halls needed to offer a new act, a new sensation, or a new partner virtually every night of the week. Not art but novelty for its own sake drove commercialisation, which in turn drove further innovation. Whereas the first moving picture show was unveiled in 1895, by 1914 there existed some 2500 cinemas in Germany with an average capacity of 200 seats. Most workers could afford to attend a movie at least once a week. Soon bicycle and motor-car races were attracting large audiences, as were soccer, boxing, and other new spectator sports [1; 4; 52; 182; 187; 268; 297].

Members of the bourgeoisie, too, increasingly took their own recreations into the public arena, attending theatres, visiting zoos, and arranging special trains to take them out of the cities. At the same time the bourgeoisie, like the SPD's own leaders, tried to ensure that workers did not dissipate their limited time and money on leisure activities without educational merit. These efforts went hand in hand with bourgeois anxiety that fashions, lifestyles, and consumerism not be associated exclusively with parvenus and philistines. For this reason one must recognise the social and political subtexts to public debates about which forms of recreation should be accessible to the masses and which should not. In fact the democratising effect of developments in popular culture remains open to interpretation. Some leisure pursuits remained very class-specific – hunting for the upper classes, pigeon-racing for workers. In comparative perspective, too, German developments did not uniformly follow patterns established elsewhere: whereas soccer emerged in England as mainly a working-class phenomenon, in Germany the cost of equipment and the lack of Sunday leisure time were among the factors preventing all but a few workers from joining soccer clubs [52].

Did a pop culture emerge in Wilhelmine Germany? Perhaps not in fully recognisable form. Yet extremely sophisticated forms of commercialisation, distribution, and marketing were certainly in place by 1914. The German masses had access to many of the cheap, 'frivolous' artefacts of modern culture that have a distinctly twentieth-century character: chain restaurants, mobile refreshment stands, pre-packaged picnic foods, mass-produced watercolours, picture postcards, and mantlepiece knick-knacks. It is less clear whether Wilhelmine culture was becoming a truly national culture. The growing importance of fads and the emergence of a star system linked to sports heroes and cinema idols certainly point in this direction. The phonograph, though available to only the privileged few, facilitated pre-war imports in dance and music: tango and ragtime arrived from the Americas, while the Berlin ditty, 'Komm, Karlineken, komm', was immediately heard in Warsaw as 'Pójdz Paulinko' and in Paris as 'Viens, poupoule' [182: p. 226]. These developments suggest that Wilhelmine popular culture was already on its way to becoming an international culture, tending toward the uniformity and blandness conjured up by the term 'McCulture'.

Whose public sphere?

Looking back over the issues addressed so far, we find that a mere enumeration of developments in either élite or popular culture does not adequately reflect the current interests of cultural historians. Taking some other issues that generated intense debate in the public sphere may reveal in different ways whether Wilhelmine Germany was an *Angst*-ridden society. What interests us is not simply the range of opinion on these subjects, but the common structures underlying the public debates they provoked. Without getting bogged down in Jürgen Habermas's detailed description of the 'public sphere' or Michel Foucault's theories of 'discourse' and 'power' [see 36; 57], a fairly simple point can be made. Studying culture and politics together can help us locate power in a given society and see who wields it, in what manner, and to what ends. Cultural history allows us to look for the operation of power outside conventionally recognised sites of political conflict. In this sense a more abstract, 'de-centred' notion of politics reveals how power was exercised in society through subtle means of social control. For the case of Wilhelmine society particularly, issues that are commonly believed to have generated an anti-modernist backlash among the bourgeoisie – the appearance of 'trash' literature, mass advertising, or sexual deviance – can now be seen as further reflections of middle-class ambivalence about 'the modern'.

The critics of 'trivial' literature faced a problem of staggering proportions. One estimate suggests that the pulp fiction available in pamphlet form in the half-decade before 1914 may have yielded revenues as high as 60 million marks per year. The principal themes and heroes were more formulaic than manipulative: wild-west stories and Nick Carter adventures, mainly. Yet these pamphlets elicited a hypersensitive reaction among moral purists. Flocking to such crusading groups as the 'People's League against Trash in Print and Picture', these critics believed the German masses were 'gripped with a kind of madness'. 'The multitude', one critic wrote, 'lunges after the gaudily-colored, enticingly-titled pamphlets as if it were under the spell of some sinister sorcerer' [86: p. 499]. Yet these moral purity leagues had little success in changing popular reading habits. The 'uplifting' reading matter they offered was excruciatingly dull and impossible to peddle, and government support for their efforts was half-hearted [269].

The emergence of a commercialised, advertisement-driven mass press after 1890 drew equally scathing attacks. Critics targeted these 'cheese-and-sausage' rags because they allegedly confused 'business' and 'principle' and thereby undermined German *Kultur*.

70

But few conservative critics of the mass press made much headway in a cultural environment that heralded the coming of age of the masses [218; 266]. The history of Germany's satirical journals also suggests that the confrontation between an inflexible political establishment and a vocal public was often oblique and ambiguous. Of these journals, the imagery of *Simplicissimus* was the most unsettling: 'risqué, violent, grotesque, even apocalyptic', it 'jolted, titillated, charmed, or frightened the reader into a confrontation with new realities'. *Simplicissimus* was none the less found in full view on middle-class coffee tables throughout Germany. Perhaps it provided an outlet for the laughter that other institutions of authority suppressed. Following Henri Bergson, Ann Taylor Allen has noted that the laugh can be a response to 'any behavior which appears puppetlike, rigid, or mechanistic'. This was exactly the pose in which cartoonists caught figures of authority: Junkers, soldiers, and the Kaiser, to be sure, but also middle-class clergy, schoolteachers, and fathers. In these caricatures, as in Heinrich Mann's fictional *Man of Straw*, rigidity was comical, and 'laughter was its punishment' [8: pp. 225–9; also 44; 165].

Very little satire in Wilhelmine Germany even came close to being pornographic. Regardless, pornography offended the same moral majority that criticised satirical attacks on authority. Every conceivable imagination could be fired by the range of pornographic materials available. In only twelve months (1904–5) the police in Munich seized no fewer than 18,000 erotic photographs and 613 varieties of postcards. When police investigated Berlin's many body-rub parlours in 1911, they were 'shocked' to discover that such parlours 'in truth did not practice massage or nail care at all' [267: pp. 205–8; also 35; 269]. Like the homosexual emancipation movement discussed earlier, pornography reflected more than just rampant sexuality and profits. It also reflected anxieties about sexual mores and gender roles. These fed the 'pleasure–power spiral' described by Foucault. As Gary Stark has observed, it was ironic that Wilhelmine censors had to drum up business to remain employed; the relationship between sexual repression and clandestine evasion was a very intimate one. Yet the danger represented by pornography did little to foster any consensus as to its root cause. Hence those outside the dominant culture were blamed, whether 'deviant' or not: the unschooled masses, the academic proletariat, fraudulent entrepreneurs,

71

homosexuals, the Jews. Only women appear to have been exempt – not because prudery and sexual repression discouraged the growth of pornography, but because the myth of women's disinterest in sex would have been exploded if gender relations were held accountable.

One final example of the 'pleasure–power' spiral is provided by the unwillingness of prostitutes to conform to the law's definition of their roles [3; 4; 64; 83: ch. 11; 131; 212; 267]. This non-conformity, too, seemed to unleash a moral panic in the 1890s. Such a panic, however, can only be understood against the backdrop of other factors that undermined the notion of a separate female sphere just when its (mythical) function was most necessary. A 'doctrine of relative obscenity' was substituted. This permitted authorities to react differently to deviance depending on how 'reputable' or 'disreputable' the target market for pornography and prostitution was. Thus, although legalised prostitution was intentionally confined to working-class neighbourhoods, bourgeois customers were allowed unimpeded access. Exhibitions showing the female sex organs or claiming to provide medical documentation of sexual diseases were not seized if they were set up in venues patronised principally by the bourgeoisie.

Pulling together the strands of this argument about cultural anxieties, their social contexts, and their political consequences, we can perhaps see two things more clearly at the end of this chapter than at the beginning. First, *all* the issues examined here were about power in one sense or another. Domination and deviance, negotiation and resistance – these provide the underlying pattern to our analysis of Wilhelmine culture no less than they do our analyses of economics, society, and politics. Second, whether Wilhelmine Germans expressed fear of 'the modern' or sought to hasten its arrival, they often did so in ways that did not help resolve underlying problems connected with the diffusion of power in society. To explore this dilemma, cultural historians have become sensitised to Wilhelmine worries about the precariousness of consensus itself. Those worries now appear as important as the objective issues being fought over. The contested nature of power and contemporaries' inability to disentangle related issues help explain why Germans reacted so ambivalently to the birth of the modern age.

3 Rattling the Sabre: *Weltpolitik* and the Great War

Structural Influences on Foreign Policy

'Bismarck had played chess; Wilhelm II played poker' [102: p. 180]. This assessment aptly endorses the usefulness of such concepts as 'bluff', 'calculated risk', and 'bid for world power' in explaining the outbreak of war in 1914. It even hints at the rapid shifts between gloom and euphoria in Berlin before the final card was played during the July crisis. Yet before we address that crisis we need to consider more broadly why the Fischer controversy remains alive. We also need to survey those structural determinants of German foreign policy that have fostered the most innovative research since the 1960s and ask what was distinctive about German decision-making.

Fritz Fischer's second book (1969) and subsequent work by his former students reveal that the 'Hamburg school' moved backward and outward from Fischer's original focus on war aims. When the 'Bielefelders' extended these analyses further, they pushed the 'primacy of domestic politics' approach with special vigour. The pressures generated by domestic impasse, it seemed, provided the most plausible explanation for the German 'escape forwards' (*Flucht nach vorn*) leading to war. But it must be remembered that the 'primacy of domestic politics' never attracted unanimous approval. The majority of historians sought the middle ground. These historians felt instinctively that a 'hardening of the categories' between domestic and foreign policy narrows the flow of scholarly dialogue. This middle ground is where the majority remain still, though German scholars remain somewhat more sceptical of Fischer's conclusions than do non-Germans [105; 128; 151; 202].

Nevertheless, present-day politics, so decisive in the original Fischer controversy, are once again challenging basic assumptions about the past. A contributing factor has been the conservative climate in the Federal Republic since Helmut Kohl became chancellor in 1981. This climate has led some conservative historians to propose a more positive, nationalist view of German history. Including the late Andreas Hillgruber, Klaus Hildebrand, Gregor Schöllgen, Lothar Gall, and Michael Stürmer, these historians recently published an English-language compendium of their arguments which considered Germany's role in the outbreak of the First World War [253]. Here the 'primacy of foreign policy' viewpoint was developed in its extreme form. Despite token essays by Fischer and a leading East German historian, the slimness of this volume reflects the exclusionary premise of the underlying viewpoint – but not its potential impact, which is considerable. These historians charge that both the Hamburg and Bielefeld 'schools' were guilty of 'relativising' history. The condemnatory tone does not end there. These historians also claim that their rivals have made an 'explicit demand for exclusivity', that their findings are 'banal', and that the social history of politics 'seems manifestly to have failed as a theoretical model and methodological concept' [mainly Schöllgen intro. in 253]. Such charges do a grave injustice to scholars of the critical school whose openness to new ideas cannot seriously be doubted.

Hence, the whole outcome of the Fischer controversy has become clouded, and all the old questions about German responsibility for war in 1914 are once again on the table. One reviewer recently noted that the 'new history' is often that of two generations earlier [74: p. 742; also intros to 17 and 18; 295: p. 247]. In German historical writing this prospect is especially chilling. Today, historians occupying the middle ground cannot ignore the possible connections between the apologist tenor of the 1950s and the fact that conservative nationalist historians refuse to put the principal blame for war on German shoulders. Such analyses seek to shift the blame elsewhere: either toward the other Great Powers or toward the abstracted international system. According to this view, alliance 'mechanisms' and Germany's 'exposed geostrategic position' were responsible for war. The 'incompatibility' of German aims with those of her rivals produced the powder keg of 1914. And foreign 'pressure' on Germany's borders, together with the inability of the other powers to cope with the unpredictability of German policy, left the Germans without 'any real alternative to the adoption of *Weltpolitik*' [253: intro. and *passim*]. We will need to return to these claims later in this chapter to consider their validity.

Little is to be gained from debating the *primacy* of foreign or domestic policy any further. Many issues still under debate cannot neatly be assigned to one sphere or the other. These include what James Joll has referred to as the 'mood of 1914'; the role of Chancellor Bethmann Hollweg and his attitude toward Britain; and the connections between industrial capitalism, imperialism, and international relations – a topic that received considerable attention from East German scholars [49; Joll *et al.* in 103; 151]. There remain three further areas of investigation, however, that also straddle the line between the domestic and foreign spheres and demonstrate the structural influence of the former on the latter. In each of these areas significant advances have been made in recent years.

1 *Armaments policy.* The 'societal function' of armaments policy was a main pillar of the primacy of domestic politics thesis [12; 19; Berghahn in 112, 132; 291]. Among many other works, Volker Berghahn's study of the 'Tirpitz plan' revealed the anti-parliamentary premise of Admiral Alfred (von) Tirpitz's quest to ensure long-term appropriations for naval construction [16; also 58]. Since early studies appeared, armaments policy has been explored from many angles, including the viability of the Schlieffen Plan, the navy's strategic planning, and the social composition of the army and navy [17; 50; 100; 101; 135]. One recent study addresses the thorny question of why German leaders appeared to possess the financial resources, but not the political will, to enlarge the army sufficiently before 1914 [75; less convincing is Dukes in 51]. This line of analysis asks whether Germany could or should have spent more on armaments. It poses an intriguing hypothesis: that German fears about encirclement and the need for a preventive strike in July 1914 would have been less extreme if the country had been *more*, not less, militaristic. This hypothesis draws attention to German economic and military performance in comparison to that of its neighbours. It addresses contemporaries' worries about 'diluting' the army with recruits of possibly non-monarchist sentiments.

75

It redirects attention back to as-yet-unanswered questions about the army's image among the middle and lower classes. It even underlines the paradox that Junkers were unwilling to sacrifice financially for the sake of the military. It is not necessary to agree fully with this particular interpretation to see that by 1914 armaments policies had placed civilian and military leaders *together* in an untenable position.

2 *Militarism*. An intense but ambiguous contemporary debate about militarism raged before 1914, both in Germany and abroad. Attacks on the Prussian officer as a bayonet-quilled porcupine in German satirical magazines were as sharp as any caricature in the foreign press. The Zabern affair of 1913, occasioned by a Prussian officer's arrogant mistreatment of civilians in the annexed province of Alsace, revealed the limits of parliament's ability to rein in the military establishment [252]. Yet the public outcry and the Reichstag's vote of non-confidence in the chancellor also revealed that the army had patently failed as the 'school of the nation'. It is in this grey area between the state and civil society that some of the most interesting research on German militarism has been conducted. Veterans associations, for example, which had a combined total of about 1.7 million members in 1910, have been studied intensively. This is also true of efforts to reform the system of military justice, the cult of duelling among students and military officers, the mentality of the reserve officer corps, campaigns to indoctrinate German youth between school-leaving age and conscription into the army, and conflicts in the public sphere between the army and the SPD [Düding in 50; 95; 120; 162; 166: ch. 3; 238; 245; 246, 248: sec. vi; 265].

Two broad conclusions emerge from this work. First, the military establishment itself was hardly as feudal, archaic, and narrow-minded as historians once believed. The Prussian army underwent a thorough professionalisation that gave priority not to traditional modes of thinking but to very modern ideals of efficiency and expertise [Showalter in 51; 54: ch. 4; 260]. Second, many middle-class Germans tended to view both the army and the navy, though with important distinctions, as fully in tune with their own values [8; 24: pp. 245–6; 38]. Over time, a consistently anti-militarist position within German liberalism became marginalised, and the 1848 ideal of an apolitical army grew less

compelling as the army's modern functions came more sharply
into view. By this reading, Wilhelmine society could be thoroughly
militarised and 'modern' at the same time. It remains to be seen
whether recent statements of this viewpoint go too far. Geoff Eley
has written that the most pugnacious militarists were not the 'up-
holders of cloistered aristocratic traditions' but the nation's most
determined modernisers. Michael Geyer has made the same point
in noting that German militarists around 1900 were not only 'uni-
formed peacocks' or fat, complacent men with duelling scars and
fake uniforms. The military functioned instead as an 'ideology'
that responded to the needs of certain segments of society. Those
who were fascinated by the cult of violence, concludes Geyer,
signed on to militarism because that cult 'extended beyond the
realm of politics into the habitus of people'. It was 'an empowering
way of life' [54: p. 102; 92: pp. 79–80].

3 *Public opinion.* Research is still very uneven on the relationship
between foreign policy and government efforts to manipulate the
press [42; 175: chs 12–14 and 16; 176: esp. pp. 207ff; 179]. To what
degree did public opinion actually constrain statesmen's freedom
of manoeuvre? Was public opinion in Germany any more chauvin-
ist than that in Britain, France, or Russia? These are still open
questions. The primacy of foreign policy advocates are correct
that decision-making in the final days of the July crisis remained
largely autonomous from the public's clamour for war. The force
of public opinion had none the less grown tremendously since
Bismarck's day. During the first Moroccan crisis of 1905–6, Chancellor Bülow wrote: 'Neither public opinion [nor] Parliament . . .
will have anything to do with war over Morocco' [128: p. 453].
Five years later during the second Moroccan crisis (1911) the opposite situation prevailed. After first whipping up public opinion
in favour of an aggressive anti-French policy and then having to
back down, Germany's leaders were badly outdistanced by the war-
mongerers. Chancellor Bethmann Hollweg's subsequent attempts
to overhaul the Reich's machinery for manipulating the press
failed badly. During the war he could only rail against the Pan-
German 'pirates of public opinion' who eventually helped topple
him from office. Even before 1914 Bethmann Hollweg was in no
doubt that Pan-German leaders 'were among the most skilled and
influential opinion-leaders in the country'. These were 'men to be

respected, despised, or feared, but certainly no longer to be ridiculed' [39: p. 283].

Weltpolitik and Battleship-building: Germany 'Encircled'

When Chancellor Caprivi took over from Bismarck in 1890, he believed he had to resolve the contradiction inherent in Germany's treaty agreements with both Austria-Hungary and Russia. When he allowed the Reinsurance Treaty with Russia to lapse, Russia gravitated toward France. The military convention of 1892 and the formal alliance of 1894 cemented their partnership. There may be good reason to ask what, if anything, the Germans could have done to prevent this. Less debatable is Germany's contribution to the alienation of its most powerful potential ally, Great Britain. There were distinct phases in this cumulative estrangement, especially 1898–1901, when Germany might have reached agreement with the British. But for too long German statesmen believed that the British would be unable to patch up their differences with the French (over African territories) and with the Russians (over a possible threat to the Indian subcontinent). The two Moroccan crises revealed the futility of German efforts to divide Britain and France with the tactic of brinkmanship. Germany's bullying of Russia during the Balkan wars of 1908–13 also created a legacy of mistrust.

Thus Europe became divided into two hostile camps. On one side stood the Triple Alliance (1882) uniting Germany, Austria-Hungary, and Italy. On the other side, the less formal Triple Entente, comprising the Franco-Russian alliance of 1894 and the *ententes cordiale* between Britain and France (1904) and Britain and Russia (1907). As German doubts grew about the resolve of Italy to fulfil her treaty obligations and about the Habsburg Empire's ability to withstand shocks coming from the Balkans, German policy became driven by the sense that *something* had to be done to break out of this ring of hostile powers. Thus the Kaiser wrote in July 1914: 'England, Russia and France have agreed among themselves . . . to take the Austro-Serbia conflict as an excuse for waging a war of extermination against us. . . . The famous encirclement of Germany has finally become a complete fact. . . . We squirm isolated in the net' [89: p. 295; also 90].

78

Wilhelm was part of the problem, not part of the solution. A major component of his 'personal regime' was established in 1897 with the appointment of Bülow as foreign secretary and Tirpitz as naval secretary. These sycophantic yes-men put a new premium on bluster and bluff in German diplomacy. Although pursued with a duplicity that was aggravating and transparent in equal measure, the remarkably vague goals of *Weltpolitik* registered the same inflated German need for self-substantiation that afflicted Wilhelm himself. In this the building of a large German navy became the central element. The Navy Bills of 1898 and 1900 reflected Wilhelm's determination to challenge Britain on a world-wide scale. This was patently a long-term project. Even Tirpitz was aware that many years would elapse before British naval supremacy could be called into question. Yet Tirpitz, Bülow, and Wilhelm hoped that after a powerful German navy was built, Britain would either not dare to enter a war in Europe involving Germany or would cut a deal that enhanced Germany's position elsewhere in the world [16; 58; 259; 299]. Of course some historians would suggest that the decision to build a German battle fleet is unthinkable without the decisive influence of a monarch known even in his day as His Impulsive Majesty and Wilhelm the Sudden. Yet the German military-industrial complex held to the 'Tirpitz plan' long after the promise of real gains had evaporated. This persistent blindness suggests that the role played by royal caprice in battleship-building should not be overemphasised.

It took Britain some time to perceive German intentions accurately and respond. By 1902, however, it had vastly escalated its own program of shipbuilding. Even the advent of the *Dreadnought* class of battleship after 1905 did not prevent the British from matching the rate at which the Germans laid new keels. Meanwhile, the German treasury found it more and more difficult to meet the phenomenal costs of the fleet. By 1906 Germany was in dire financial straits: despite agreements with the British on imperial issues of secondary importance, by 1912 at the latest *Weltpolitik* was in shambles too. If a cost–benefit analysis of *Weltpolitik* had been sought by either the German public or German statesmen – the great tragedy is that it was sought by neither – it would have shown that this scheme was based mainly on wishful thinking. As one military commander had written even in the 1890s: 'We are supposed to pursue *Weltpolitik*. If only we knew what it is supposed

79

to be' [101: p. 20]. And so, quietly, *Weltpolitik* was relegated to the back burner. Continental aims re-emerged as the first priority. The Army Bills of 1912–13 reflected the growing awareness that Germany's fate would be decided in a two-front war against France and Russia. Yet even these bills failed to match the manpower increases legislated by France and Russia. When news of an impending naval agreement between Britain and Russia reached Bethmann Hollweg in June 1914, he described this as 'the last link in the chain'. Just one week before the assassination of the Austrian heir to the throne by a Serbian nationalist on 28 June 1914, Wilhelm asked 'whether it would not be better to strike now, rather than wait'.

The July Crisis

The larger interpretative models historians use still determine how they view the motives and mentalities that shaped the crisis of 1914. Between his first and second books, Fischer radicalised his interpretation of Germany's bid for world power. Eventually he argued that from the time of a now-famous 'war council' between Wilhelm and his military advisors in December 1912, Germany was looking for the first opportunity to unleash a war of aggression on her enemies [77: ch. 9]. Few historians endorse this conclusion. Most still prefer the idea that Bethmann Hollweg undertook a 'calculated risk' to shore up Germany's diplomatic position [103; 115; 116]. The goal was to split the Entente, provide Austria-Hungary with a prestigious *coup* in the Balkans, and rally public opinion. This was to be done without a general European conflict or, if one did come, with Britain remaining neutral. This risk was closely tied up with the double illusion of a limited war: the illusion that the general pattern of German diplomacy – limited risks and limited aims – could be continued, and the illusion that the next war would approximate the lightning campaigns of 1864, 1866, and 1870.

The calculated risk went badly wrong – though by instalments. On 5 July the Germans issued a so-called 'blank cheque' to the Austrians, urging them to deal with the Serbian threat as they saw fit. The Austrian ultimatum was not finally delivered to the Serbs until 23 July, at which point the British intervened for peace. Until 28 July, Bethmann's delaying tactics masked German complicity. Thereafter, a last flurry of negotiations was complicated by a temporary loss of nerve by the Kaiser. Bethmann's overriding concern was to await Russian mobilisation in defence of Serbian interests. Only if Russia mobilised first, Bethmann felt, would the German government have any hope of persuading Britain to remain neutral. Even more important, Bethmann had to exploit the Social Democrats' fear of the Tsarist autocracy to the east to persuade them to support a 'defensive war'. It was *this* 'calculation' that monopolised Bethmann's thoughts as all options for peace disappeared and general mobilisations began.

Scholars still disagree about even the calculated risk theory. Few historians any longer hold to the comforting view of Bethmann Hollweg as an indecisive but valiant civilian leader who succumbed to the General Staff's demand for war – 'the sooner the better', as Chief of Staff Helmuth von Moltke (the Younger) put it. Yet the blank cheque to Austria could be cashed only if it were countersigned by both the chancellor and the Kaiser, and both men appeared determined to oppose 'go-for-broke' policies as long as possible. Volker Berghahn, Konrad Jarausch, and Wolfgang J. Mommsen are among those who still believe that civilian–military conflicts in Berlin frustrated Bethmann's attempts to find a diplomatic solution. Paradoxically, this accords with their inclination to give great weight to domestic factors: not because Bethmann thought a war of aggression would be popular or would remove the threat of revolution at home – he knew better – but because domestic stalemate had reduced Bethmann's authority and decisiveness. As Berghahn has recently written, Bethmann Hollweg by July 1914 'had virtually given up governing' [18: p. 292; Mayer *et al.* in 103; 116: p. 240; 175: p. 312].

Compelling evidence can be mustered, however, for an alternative conclusion. This suggests that the calculated risk theory still ascribes too much innocence and too little aggressiveness to this not-so-enigmatic chancellor [113]. Ironically, domestic policy is a key component of this alternative scenario too. By this reading, Bethmann Hollweg no more faced deadlock at home than had any of his predecessors. Socialist victories in the Reichstag elections of 1912 had not destroyed political stability, as many observers had originally feared. Moreover, by 1914 Bethmann Hollweg had effectively marginalised the Conservatives, who had proved to be Bülow's undoing [Retallack in 126]. On the other hand, the chancellor's foreign policy outlook may have been darker (though also more proactive) than the calculated risk theory has it. Far *more* than his predecessor, Bethmann Hollweg had begun to believe the rhetoric of *Weltpolitik* about Germany's 'need' to expand and about the coming showdown between Slavs and Teutons [see esp. 128: p. 463]. Having been worn down by Moltke's insistence that Germany could still win a preventive war against both her neighbours, news of Anglo-Russian naval discussions convinced the chancellor that his patient efforts to ensure British neutrality had come to naught. What was his reaction? In contrast to a picture of a fatalistic Bethmann Hollweg standing frozen in the glare of the coming apocalypse, Fritz Fischer has recently written that during the crisis 'the Chancellor was, in fact, a bundle of energy and activity' [253: p. 31]. Agreeing with Fischer's version of events, John Röhl has written that the calculated risk theory 'was either not calculated at all, or . . . was calculated to produce a war'. Furthermore, adds Röhl, 'to apply the adjective "preventive" to a war begun because of vague pessimistic prognostications . . . is to depart a long way from the original meaning of that term' [103: pp. 100–1].

Historians will continue to debate the degree to which Bethmann Hollweg may have moved toward the camp of hardliners. The reader is invited to reach his or her own conclusions from the evidence. This synoptic account has tried not to conflate the different illusions under which civilian and military leaders entered the July crisis. Nor should it be denied that the responsibility for war was both individual and collective – on one level. Nevertheless, one central question that confronted Fritz Fischer in 1961 still commands our attention too: can German policy in 1914 be legitimised – not just explained – by any real threat to German security? The answer here must surely be no. German perceptions of encirclement may have been real enough. But the 'threat' itself was not, for no reputable historian would now claim that the Entente planned to attack Germany [202]. This conclusion reinforces not just the kernel of Fischer's original thesis but its moral impact too. The calculated risk theory might still be accepted as 'a reasonable explanation of Bethmann's less than reasonable conduct' [151: p. 177]. But to construe the 'calculated risk' as just another badly *miscalculated* risk, as just another failed exercise in brinkmanship, would be to claim that Germany's larger ambitions – hegemony on the continent and parity with the British world-wide – were perfectly legitimate and *not* unreasonable. This in turn would endorse the conservative nationalist view outlined earlier and signify a retreat to the pre-Fischer position of the 1950s.

The Horror in Flanders, the Misery at Home

From the Heidelberger Platz onward, the streets were black with people. . . . The tension grew. People thought they heard distant drum-beats. A wave of shouts rolled along the streets. . . . And now the trumpets were indeed approaching.

And then came the sight that caused many in the crowd to weep. Men as well as women, moved by a feeling of humanity's common fate, remembering the long war and all the dead.

Did the people see the troops? They were looking at the long war, at victories and at the defeats. Before them a piece of their own life was marching past, with wagons and horses, machine-guns and cannons. [Döblin in 20: p. v]

Most accounts of Germany's first experience of total war begin by re-creating the patriotic exultation of August 1914. But Alfred Döblin's account of German soldiers returning home in December 1918 reflects the same dimension of war from a different angle, stressing the combined effect of military and personal traumas.

On 4 August 1914 Wilhelm declared that 'I no longer recognise parties; I recognise only Germans.' This was wishful thinking again. The notion of a domestic political truce (*Burgfrieden*) was based on the idea that class antagonisms, party squabbles, and other cleavages in German society could be conjured out of existence. But it rested on two mistaken assumptions: that the war would be a short one, and that it would bring a meaningful victory. The 'spirit of August 1914' revealed mainly that the *outbreak* of war provided temporary relief from peace-time tensions. Even the Social Democrats saw their moderate, evolutionary program of working with the German state confirmed by the call to arms. As one of their leaders noted his diary in August 1914, suffrage reform in Prussia would be picked as a fruit of the conflict. To achieve that end, 'we are fighting a war instead of a general strike' [192: vol. 2, p. 783].

The patriotic consensus of August 1914 was not as complete as historians once thought. Research has revealed that some sections of the population had been inoculated against war hysteria by pacifist teaching or class solidarity [285]. In any case, the consensus could only survive if the army proved victorious. But the German invasion of France halted in the second week of September at the Battle of the Marne. Although advance German units were able to see the Eiffel Tower in Paris, the Schlieffen Plan's anticipated swing around Paris to encircle the French army was badly undercut by insufficient manpower and Moltke's faint-heartedness. By Christmas 1914 an ugly black scrawl of trenches stretched from Switzerland to the English Channel. That line moved very little until the summer of 1918 despite repeated attempts at breakthrough by all combatants. During those four years some 10.6 million German males were scarred in one way or another by wartime service [20: p. 6].

The knock-out blow could not be delivered on any other front either. The war against Russia initially went favourably. The Battle of Tannenberg in the late summer of 1914 routed the Russians and established the reputations of Paul von Hindenburg and Erich Ludendorff. But no military decision in the east ensued. During the naval Battle of Jutland in 1916, the German fleet inflicted heavier damage on the British navy than it suffered itself; but Tirpitz's High Seas Fleet did not dare to venture out of port again. One year later, German unrestricted submarine warfare had contributed to America's entry into the war. By the spring of 1918 American arms and *matériel* had tipped the military balance against Germany. This more than matched the increase in German manpower in the west resulting from Russia's exit from the war after the Bolshevik revolution in October 1917.

The military impasse in 1914 had sent domestic politics in an authoritarian direction. Economic reform came first. Under the guidance of men like the banker Karl Helfferich and the industrial manager Walther Rathenau, economic planning was quickly centralised. The principal feature of the so-called Hindenburg Program, designed finally to mobilise Germany for total war, was the Auxiliary Service Law of 5 December 1916. This tried to reconcile the conflicting interests of heavy industry and labour (especially skilled labour). Although this program virtually conscripted labour, it also made trade unions accepted partners in economic decision-making. This undercuts the thesis that Hindenburg and Ludendorff exerted a 'silent dictatorship' after 1916. Most historians now believe that this term is too categorical in suggesting a concentration of power that did not actually exist [12; 71; 136].

Meanwhile the democratisation that liberals and socialists hoped for was repeatedly postponed. Reichstag deputies refused to be marginalised completely. In July 1917 the parties Bismarck had designated 'enemies of the state' – the socialists, Progressives, and Centre – resolved to extend peace feelers to the Allies. But the right's outraged reaction to such 'defeatism' was the same as it had been the previous February when Bethmann Hollweg announced he would consider reforming Prussia's three-class suffrage. Even before the Reichstag debated the peace resolution of 1917, Bethmann had been toppled by the army high command. He was replaced as chancellor by an obscure bureaucrat named Georg Michaelis, who later in the war made way for Georg von Hertling and then, at the eleventh hour, for Prince Max of Baden. Such ministerial shuffles could not mask the fact that the *Burgfrieden* was no longer viable. Even individual parties were riven by the pressures of war. The Conservative leadership was barely able to resist Pan-German sympathisers within the party. On the left the SPD was fractured in 1917 by the secession of radicals who formed the Independent Social Democratic Party (USPD). This party disagreed with the Majority SPD's increasingly close collaboration with the capitalist German state. It also called for immediate peace without annexations. But in contrast to the Spartacists around Rosa Luxemburg and Karl Liebknecht, who stood even further to the left, the USPD was not in favour of violent revolution [79; 186; 214: ch. 15; 254].

By 1917 it was impossible to overlook the widening gulf between those who sought a 'peace without victory' and those who believed that only a 'victorious peace' (*Siegfrieden*) would legitimate the sacrifices already made. A victorious peace would be not only vengeful but expansionist. For this reason it was supported by industrialists who coveted rich iron-ore deposits in France and

85

Belgium, by Junkers who looked to the vast grain-growing steppes of Russia to realise their vision of an expanded agrarian state, and by Pan-Germans who sought to unite all Germans outside the borders of the Reich. Scholars still disagree about how Bethmann Hollweg and his successors regarded the war-aims movement. Some say they endorsed this expansionist program wholeheartedly; others say they resisted it as a dangerous illusion; still others suggest that they hoped for moderate gains consistent with the pre-war goals of German *Weltpolitik*. Recall that Fritz Fischer initially suggested that Germany went to war to realise this expansionist programme. This led Fischer to argue that German wartime imperialism was close enough to the Nazi dream of *Lebensraum* for Bethmann Hollweg to be called the 'Hitler of 1914'. Bethmann should not be tarred with the same brush as Hitler. Nevertheless, Bethmann's waning authority and continuing hopes for annexations made German leaders deaf to suggestions for a peace based on the *status quo ante*. Even as the tide of war turned, many Germans were still determined to exact their vengeful peace. This was signalled by the appearance of the German Fatherland Party in mid-1917 and the draconian Treaty of Brest-Litovsk with the Russians the following March. Although Brest-Litovsk fuelled the Allies' determination to make Germany pay for the costs of the war, it also fed hopes on the German right that similar gains might be made in the west.

Such hopes could not diminish the significance of war-weariness and malnutrition at home. Strikes for higher wages broke out in April 1917 and January 1918. The 'turnip winter' of 1916–17 was followed by far greater suffering and political unrest a year later. Together with a series of monstrous influenza outbreaks in 1918, this unrest revealed the depth of human misery and declining morale on the home front [192: vol. 2, sec. vi.6]. Yet no groundswell for political reform arose until the final months of the war, partly due to National Liberal ambivalence [232; 240]. And so the German people suffered on, unable to make the leap in the dark toward full democracy until the last weeks of the war.

When reform finally came, it did so with a suddenness born of waiting. By the end of October 1918, Germany was effectively a parliamentary monarchy with Wilhelm II as a ceremonial figurehead. When the army command finally admitted that military defeat loomed and when the prospect of total collapse dawned on the German public, a naval mutiny broke out in Kiel on 29 October. Kurt Eisner led a Bolshevik-style revolution in Munich on 8 November. The Reichstag always seemed to be one step behind events; but the people's desperate desire for peace could not be resisted. On 9 November things came to a head. The prominent SPD politician Philipp Scheidemann was lunching in the Reichstag when he heard a rumour that the Spartacist Karl Liebknecht was about to proclaim a socialist republic. Quickly wiping his mouth, Scheidemann rushed onto the Reichstag balcony and, to tumultuous applause, proclaimed a 'German Republic' (he did not, however, define exactly what sort of republic it would be). That same afternoon Max of Baden announced the abdication of the Kaiser and handed over the reins of power to the SPD's Friedrich Ebert. After quick negotiations with the USPD, Ebert formed a governing Council of People's Commissars. That evening Ebert also concluded a famous telephone pact with General Wilhelm Groener whereby the SPD and army high command pledged their joint resolve to avoid a civil war, prevent a Bolshevik revolution, and maintain the command powers of the officer corps. On 10 November Kaiser Wilhelm crossed the border to Holland on his way to a lengthy and well-deserved exile, and peace finally broke out on 11 November. In the meantime, Hindenburg and Ludendorff had successfully shifted the odium of peace-making onto the shoulders of civilian leaders. They thereby contributed, quite intentionally, to the 'stab in the back' legend that Germany was defeated by unrest at home, not on the battlefield.

Recent studies have generated relatively few new insights about the military or diplomatic course of the war. Even the realm of domestic politics has lately tended to produce variations on familiar themes, although historians continue to debate the importance of 'radical' or 'non-radical' indicators of grass-roots sentiments among the working classes during the November revolution [Geary in 67; 203]. The effects of Germany's fiscal irresponsibility during the war has been another area of major concern. Yet these issues are viewed increasingly from a perspective that focuses on the social upheavals caused by the war. New evidence about class conflict, gender relations, and family life are leading historians to re-evaluate many previous assumptions about the German experience of war.

Economic mobilisation for total war had unanticipated social consequences. Because many Germans were excluded from decision-making or profit-taking, they nurtured understandable grievances about the uneven distribution of suffering on the homefront. In middle-class ranks particularly, the war produced stark contrasts between winners and losers: one's indispensability to the war effort determined one's status. Of course we should not conflate Wilhelmine and Weimar examples of 'social hypochondria' – the ability of certain groups to complain without really suffering [22: ch. 5; also 194]. The fact that this malady was attributed by one left liberal to the Agrarian League in the 1890s reveals that the middle classes had been infected long before 1914. Yet the war does seem to have dramatically worsened both the immediate symptoms and the long-term prognosis.

Jürgen Kocka's pioneering study of class conflict during the war addressed this problem directly [137]. Kocka has been accused of using models too abstractly and offering an overly rigid structural analysis of society. In fact his conclusion that German society was dramatically polarised by the war deserves attention. So does his intriguing hypothesis that artisans and certain other members of the old *Mittelstand* came to see their interests lying with industrialists in resisting state intervention and limiting the new political power of the proletariat. White-collar workers, civil servants, and other members of the new *Mittelstand*, on the other hand, increasingly recognised their community of interest with manual labourers [137: pp. 111–12]. If this is true, perhaps we need to reconsider the accepted belief that the old *Mittelstand* was gradually sinking in status during the Wilhelmine era and the new *Mittelstand* was rising. Kocka nevertheless lays too much stress on the magnitude of the gulf that divided the winners and losers in wartime society [compare 137: p. 99; 175: p. 447; 192: vol. 2, pp. 799–800]. This leads him to suggest that the *Mittelstand* was polarised during the war and that Germany by 1918 was on the way to becoming a two-class society.

Other historians believe that to speak of 'the' *Mittelstand* at all is misleading (see also Chapter 4). Instead we should examine elements of the *Mittelstand* on the basis of regional or sectoral analyses. We must also appreciate the tensions felt *jointly* by (partial) winners and (partial) losers within its ranks. Those tensions were based largely on perceived discrepancies within the middle classes or between them and the working classes. The spectre of middle-class proletarisation, in other words, probably had far more effect than the reality. When contemporaries were confronted with massive social changes occurring in the space of only a few years, they assessed the costs of the war in terms of human misery, loss of former status, and new worries about the future. Those assessments may not tally exactly with the balance sheets usually drawn up by historians.

Gender relations are a case in point. Some historians have argued that women's participation in the workforce did not increase much at all, or merely continued prewar trends. Yet a modest global increase should not be taken as evidence that dramatic shifts in female employment *within* the total female labour force did not occur. In fact women flooded into war industries [Daniel in 79; 83: ch. 13; 192: vol. 2, pp. 798–9; Daniel in 288]. Of course many contemporaries regarded a shift of gender roles as a purely temporary measure – an uncomfortable response to an emergency situation. The gains registered by women workers during the war were limited, and many women were forced to retreat from the workforce after 1918 [Domansky in 57; 61: ch. 5; Usborne in 288]. These developments helped establish trends that became far more burdensome for women during the Weimar Republic and the Third Reich. Yet there is no inherent reason to suppose that the modest self-empowerment of German women came to a sudden halt in 1914. At least for some women, the war enhanced their ability to improve their material lot and public roles. There is no evidence that anything comparable occurred to the benefit of German women during the Second World War.

The history of the German family is another area where recent research on the war is making tremendous strides. Demographically and in terms of hygiene and health, the revolutionary effects of total war are plain to see. The government's success in streamlining armaments production contrasted sharply with its inability to supply civilians with sufficient food and medical provisions. As the Allied blockade drew tighter after 1916, German civilians, though they did not starve *en masse*, did suffer severe malnutrition and infectious diseases that made life, for most, truly miserable [20: pp. 33–42; Triebel in 288]. The sustenance and health crises were accompanied by a perceived moral crisis. As women became the head of the household in millions of families, older patterns of authority no longer operated [279; Wall and Reulecke in 288]. The

89

resulting traumas of generational conflict, the cult of the male, and the 'myth of the trenches' have too easily been ascribed to the experience of trench warfare exclusively. The dark shadow these problems cast over the 1920s bears the same outline as other tensions generated by the interaction of home and front. More important still, the inability of the state to cushion the young, the old, and the sick from harsh wartime realities was open for all to see. In 1915, just when food was becoming scarce, a group of women presented an anonymous petition to the Hamburg Senate that asked pointedly: 'So where is the government of Hamburg?' [79: p. 89].

Rather than emphasising the *lack* of upheaval caused by the war, therefore, it would seem more legitimate to stress how few Germans were expecting the sudden shocks to the system after 1914 [Robson in 125]. Germans may have reacted to those shocks by seeking familiar, even conservative, solutions to their problems after the war. But the disorientation occasioned by the war was revolutionary in its own right, as Richard Bessel has recently suggested:

> At stake were neither just economic and class interests nor simply the power of the military and state bureaucracy, but also social values – conceptions of a just society and of 'normal' social relations which the War had allegedly disrupted. . . . The War had bankrupted the old regime in every sense. [20: p. 48]

Perhaps a cautionary note should be sounded when the November 1918 revolution is described as the exact opposite of a 'true' social revolution or politically 'stillborn'. In late October 1918 the National Liberal leader Gustav Stresemann already saw the coming upheaval as the consequence of an unbridgable gap between *Volk* and state [72: pp. 527–8; see also 240].

Where exactly does this reading of events leave us? The constitutional changes inaugurated in 1918–19 were not primarily the consequence of class polarisation or escalating political conflict. Rather, the revolution broke out because the state, besides failing to defend national security, also failed to satisfy or protect its citizens' socio-economic well-being. More precisely: it failed to protect their *sense* of well-being [e.g. 11: p. 119; Ullrich in 79; 137: ch. 4; 175: chs 17 and 18; 192: vol. 2, sec. vi.2]. When Germans during the war cried out for assistance in the face of profiteering, hoarding, black-market dealing, and other forms of corruption, the state discovered that it could not defend both producers and consumers. In the cities, where officials could not ensure even the bare necessities of life, no amount of redistributive ingenuity could meet the twin challenge of social and political protest. In the countryside, efforts to streamline production and distribution elicited equally outraged protests from farmers: the new interventionist state was 'confiscating' their goods [170]. Thus the war frustrated the efforts of all Germans, but on many different fronts. It undermined the state's aura of legitimacy; yet it also undercut the efforts of those who sought to challenge state authority. The war did not heighten class conflict to the point that class completely obscured cleavages based on region, gender, ethnicity, religion, or ideology. Nevertheless, even as the November revolution unfolded, the just society that might have helped mask or ameliorate these divisions was already receding into the distance. Although it had withstood many challenges to its legitimacy, in November 1918 German authoritarianism became obsolete; the deep divisions within German society, however, did not. At the same instant that Wilhelmine Germany passed into the history books, the frustrations, resentments, and disunity generated by its wartime collapse became the hallmarks of political discourse in the new republic.

4 The Many Germanies of Wilhelm II

Whereas Chapter 2 addressed the diversity of Wilhelmine Germany from economic, social, political, and cultural perspectives, this chapter considers the principal social groupings in more detail. German society after 1890 was a more mature and dynamic society than in the age of Bismarck. But because of this it was also more fractured and conflict-ridden. This chapter, although organised to survey the social scale from top to bottom, seeks to reveal the complexity of both *inter*-class and *intra*-class relations. It also suggests how historians are grappling with the problem of extrapolating from studies of individual classes to discover larger patterns of social change.

Kaiser Wilhelm, the Court, and the Prussian Junkers

The flood of scholarship in the 1960s and 1970s largely relegated Kaiser Wilhelm II to the sidelines. He became something of an 'unperson', obscured by the impersonal forces and complex structures of history. 'Wilhelminism', wrote Wehler in 1973, is 'a term often used quite inappropriately to sum up this era. . . . It was not Wilhelm II who imposed his will on government policy during this period, but the traditional oligarchies in conjunction with the anonymous forces of an authoritarian polycracy' [291: pp. 64, 274]. John Röhl and others, by contrast, have stressed the many roles Wilhelm played in society and politics. It should be noted that both Röhl and Wehler were concerned with high politics. But in a pioneering volume on the Kaiser published in 1982, Röhl argued that concentration on court society need not neglect

92

theory or structures. The 'kingship mechanism', the 'palace perspective', and the 'role strain' inherent in Wilhelm's ceremonial duties, Röhl observed, all illustrate how personalities and structures in history complement one another. Röhl also argued that 'polycratic chaos' and the Kaiser's 'personal rule' need not be mutually exclusive. Wilhelm's restless nature and his unpredictable influence on policy could well have caused the power vacuum Wehler identified [Röhl in 235; also 108; 234].

Biographies of Kaiser Wilhelm have flooded the market in recent years, with more to follow in the near future. In both life and death Kaiser Wilhelm continues to serve as a kind of lightning rod, attracting controversy but not entirely discharging it [22: ch. 2; 55; 60: ch. 2; more recently, 180]. The most useful works on Wilhelm II continue to inform our understanding of his times. One example is Kathcrine Lerman's study of Chancellor Bülow, the 'courtly sycophant' [158]. Lerman's study now offers the best introduction to high politics in the period 1900–9. Such studies work a rich vein of untapped archival documents that will remain crucial sources for historians working on very different topics.

Thomas Kohut has recently used the metaphor of a mirror to stress Wilhelm's relationship with German society. Seeking to integrate Prussia's authoritarian past with Germany's present and future, Wilhelm understood (however murkily) that German society was changing rapidly. When the Kaiser wore the traditional Prussian spiked helmet (*Pickelhaube*) to the opening of a modern institute of technology, he expected no offence to be taken – and none was [142: pp. 159–62]. Yet such accounts must be balanced against the many occasions when quite the opposite reaction resulted. When Wilhelm visited Munich in September 1891, his entry in the city's guest book – '*Suprema lex regis voluntas esto*' ('Let the king's will be the highest law') – evoked a storm of public protest. That storm grew as the Kaiser's expressions of autocratic power became more frequent and more embarrassing. We must therefore bear in mind the multiplicity of German conceptions of monarchy. Nevertheless, the notion that the monarch mirrored the hopes and fears of his subjects may help reconcile two images of Wilhelmine Germany whose proximity is matched only by their discordance. As Kohut has noted, Wilhelm incorporated contradictory elements within himself and reflected them back on German society. In both cases traditionalism and modernity were

93

integrated 'only insofar as they were fragments of the same incoherent personality' [142: p. 162; also 165; 191: p. 174; Fehrenbach in 235; 262: ch. 2].

Critics have noted that Wilhelm's biographers often fail to practise what they preach. They sometimes display a marked *lack* of interest in the structures of history. Thus we are treated to gruesome stories of Empress Victoria's amateur attempts to repair the damage to Prince Wilhelm's left arm, and we even learn about Wilhelm's preference for generals and courtiers willing to dress up as ballerinas and poodles to amuse him. But this hardly substantiates Röhl's reformulated thesis that Wilhelm exercised personal rule 'in the negative sense' [55; 234]. All too often we are told nothing concrete about the policies actually undertaken by Wilhelm's capriciously chosen men. Similarly, the evolution of power relationships among the top players remains mysteriously static. Despite Isabel Hull's study of the Kaiser's immediate entourage, the influence of the chiefs of Wilhelm's military, naval, and civil cabinets has yet to be investigated in detail [108]. For these reasons one reviewer hit the mark when he wrote that some early accounts of the Kaiser and his court offered 'a baffling mixture of aperçu and cliché, insight and silliness' [22: p. 48].

Although our understanding of how nobilities and court societies actually functioned has been augmented recently through comparative investigations [see 255], our knowledge of rural society remains woefully incomplete. Hans Rosenberg set out to write a social history of Prussia's landed nobility, the Junkers, but despite a promising beginning never completed this daunting task. Not a single monograph has appeared on the Bavarian, Saxon, Mecklenburg, or Baden nobility either. We have hardly progressed beyond Max Weber's contemporary observations (1895) about the implications of defending a traditional power élite that had already been reduced to little more than an agrarian capitalist class [174: pp. 35–40]. The novels of Theodore Fontane – *Effi Briest* and *Der Stechlin*, for example – still provide the best entrée into this uncharted historiographical terrain.

The liabilities of trying to shoe-horn a history of rural society into a political account of German conservatism are clear [Puhle and Schissler in 173; see also 126]. Nevertheless, the inability of the Prussian Junkers to play the historical role of the British lords has not induced historians to neglect either Weber's remarks in

94

1895 or those of his contemporary, Friedrich Naumann, who referred to the typical Junker as an 'authoritarian type [*Herren-mensch*] with democratic gloves'. The Junkers' ruthless survival instinct became a key component of Germany's alleged *Sonderweg*. According to this view, the British nobility by 1914 had already begun to wave the white flag of economic decline as a class, voluntarily submitting to their own demise. But the German Junkers were anomalous. They could not, or would not, read the writing on the wall, and therefore fought ruthlessly to preserve their many privileges. The political consequences of this were enormous. As Alexander Gerschenkron put it in 1943, the price of bread and the fate of democracy in Germany were connected. By preserving the power of the Junkers on their landed estates in the east, German history was encumbered with a fateful legacy. Hans Rosenberg stressed how the Junkers' 'pseudo-democratisation' allowed them to incorporate modern techniques of mass politics to achieve very unmodern aims [Rosenberg in 112]. When combined with state support in the form of protective tariffs, this strategy allowed the Junkers to survive in an uncongenial age.

This view is no longer uncritically accepted. The conception of the German nobility (or even the Prussian nobility alone) as a single class does not hold water [29; 126; Dipper in 155; Reif in vol. 4 of 249; 255]. Nor do many historians still believe that the Junkers unilaterally mobilised rural discontent to serve their narrow class interests. Instead, the Junkers' attempt to win mass support was a desperate act of *containment* – a strategy that could be only partially implemented in circumstances the Junkers had not created [Eley in 126; 214: pt ii]. Economic historians now emphasise the way German agriculture as a whole, not just the Junker class, adapted to modern economic forces. This relativises Wehler's picture of galling social and economic inequalities. Lastly, extreme anti-Semitism, radical nationalism, and anti-socialism were more broadly diffused throughout German society than historians once believed. This further undermines early accounts of Junker success in *imposing* anti-democratic and anti-modern values on German society from above.

It is difficult to say precisely how far in the other direction the pendulum has swung. One economic historian recently suggested that it is a mistake to label protective tariffs a brutal act of 'state-supported agrarian–heavy-industrial perfidy' [99: p. 200]. Thomas

Nipperdey, too, has suggested an alternative view of Germany's landowning élite that is more nuanced. Nipperdey's élite has room for the 'cabbage Junker', the 'consumption-oriented debt-maker', the 'capitalist' and the 'paternalist', the 'conventional' Junker and the 'outcast', the old conservative, the new conservative, and even the liberal conservative. Nipperdey, in short, wants us to see not only 'ignorant lords and caste mentalities' but also 'polished, delightful, and original figures from an older world' [192: vol. 1, p. 213]. By any measure this view is unmistakably more positive – some would say flattering – than the consensus of only a few years ago.

The Educated and Propertied Bourgeoisie

Geoff Eley and David Blackbourn stirred considerable controversy in 1980 when they first argued that the German bourgeoisie (*Bürgertum*) was as influential as the aristocracy in the social and economic spheres, though still disadvantaged in the realm of politics [24]. This argument formed a key component of their onslaught against the idea of a German *Sonderweg*. Rather than seeing Nazism as the result of the German bourgeoisie's failure to effect a political revolution comparable to those in England in the seventeenth century or in France in 1789, Blackbourn and Eley argued that bourgeois revolutions can occur in other guises. Such revolutions may bring to ascendancy bourgeois manners, laws, and economies, even while helping mould a political system that falls far short of the liberal democratic ideal (as Wilhelmine Germany clearly did). Nor are bourgeois revolutions necessarily either sudden or violent. Quite the contrary, they may be most successful where they are least noticed: the process of establishing bourgeois hegemony may be a very drawn-out affair. This line of argument suggests that further study of bourgeois society might hold the key to understanding what changed, rather than what remained static, during the empire.

Until recently there was a dearth of research on the German bourgeoisie. Even in 1991 Gerhard A. Ritter noted – perhaps inaccurately, at that point – that this work was still in its infancy [224:

p. 48]. Until the 1980s, the German bourgeoisie was generally depicted as 'a supine class, genuflecting to the authoritarian state, aping the social values and manners of the aristocracy, lacking in civic spirit and political engagement' [25: p. 1]. But during the second half of the 1980s, work on the German bourgeoisie represented the single most important stimulus to Wilhelmine scholarship, especially in bringing comparative insights to bear in a sustained manner [84; 139; 140; 141]. Much of this research was initially conducted at the Center for Interdisciplinary Research in Bielefeld. As a result of this enterprise and related research projects, the whole nature of society and culture in pre-1914 Germany has undergone a profound reassessment. This may seem ironic given that the bourgeoisie made up no more than about 5 per cent of the German population around 1900. Yet it should already be apparent that this social group had a historical influence out of all proportion to its numerical strength.

The Bielefeld project organised its investigations along three principal lines.

1 It attempted, first, to define the *Bürgertum* and its principal components. From about the middle of the nineteenth century onward, the word *Bürgertum* was used to refer to only the more affluent and 'independent' portions of the middle classes (a grouping previously referred to *en bloc* as either the *Mittelstand* or the *Stadtbürgertum*). The designation *Bürgertum* thus corresponds roughly to the French *bourgeoisie* (including the *haute* but not the *petite bourgeoisie*) and the English term 'upper-middle classes'. The term *Mittelstand* came to be reserved for what the French call the *petite bourgeoisie*, what the English call the petty bourgeoisie or lower-middle classes, and what the Germans – to compound the confusion – call the *Kleinbürgertum*. In any case, once this *Mittelstand/Bürgertum* distinction had been demarcated, yet another distinction arose during the last half of the century.

Within the bourgeoisie, this distinction divided what might be termed the 'thinkers' and the 'makers' [Blackbourn in 25]. The 'thinkers' were the older component of the bourgeoisie: academically trained state officials, professors, Protestant clergy, professionals (doctors, lawyers, engineers, scientists), and others whose status was based largely on higher learning. The explosion

97

of state bureaucracies, university enrolments, and the professions ensured that this educated bourgeoisie retained considerable social status up to 1914 [43; 140: pt iii; 287]. The German ideals of education and 'cultivation' (*Bildung*) supported such claims to social leadership.

The advance of the educated bourgeoisie was none the less outstripped by the rise of the economic bourgeoisie – the 'makers'. The fact that this group is referred to as the 'economic', 'propertied', or 'grand' bourgeoisie (*Wirtschafts-*, *Besitz-*, or *Großbürgertum*) calls attention to its combined social and economic prominence. (Its members' relatively great wealth can be measured by Rudolf Martin's twenty-volume *Yearbook of German Millionaires* dating from 1911 [esp. 13; 127].) These were the entrepreneurs and upper managers of industry, bankers, merchants, and other commercial interests. Together they supplied the investments, the talent, and the drive behind the first and second industrial revolutions. Those engaged in large-scale manufacturing set the tone early on. But the development of the tertiary sector (banking, shipping, insurance, and large-scale retail enterprises) later introduced a new style and range of interests within this group.

Research on the bourgeoisie, in short, reveals just how finely textured the ranks of the bourgeoisie actually were. One of the most important findings of the Bielefeld project underlined the *lack* of a single 'class interest' uniting this group. From this some historians have gone on to argue that it is virtually impossible to adduce a common political outlook among such a fractured social group. Others, however, believe that a homogenising trend became apparent in the late imperial period, when external threats – for example, the rise of socialism – tended to flatten out disparities of outlook within the bourgeoisie.

2 The Bielefeld project also revealed the important connections between the bourgeoisie's amazing success story and the emergence of modern 'civil society' (*bürgerliche Gesellschaft*). Responding in part to the challenge thrown down by Blackbourn and Eley, this research examined the development of the German public sphere and the degree to which it expanded or contracted social opportunities for certain middle-class groups (especially women, Jews, and Catholics). Despite tremendous advance on some fronts, this research has left many areas virtually untouched. For example, little

work has been done on the German press and the extent to which it educated the German *Bürger* to be a responsible *Staatsbürger* analogous to the French *citoyen*. Many participants in these research projects have also noted that relations between the bourgeoisie and the state need to be investigated in greater detail and with more attention to regional disparities.

3   A third feature of the Bielefeld project was its exploration of the concept of '*Bürgerlichkeit*'. A difficult term, *Bürgerlichkeit* refers to 'the extent to which middle-class values and interests altered the texture of nineteenth century European society' [preface, Frevert, Kocka, Tilly, and Vogel in 141]. The advances made in this area of investigation justify David Blackbourn's recent observation that works dealing with Wilhelmine Germany consider it as part of a European bourgeois epoch with a 'naturalness that would have been unthinkable twenty years ago' [25: p. 2]. A list of the most important features of *Bürgerlichkeit* would emphasise two related aspects: a widely held faith in the just rewards of hard work, struggle, and achievement; and the need to live by rules. Such rules included the rule of law, but also proper table manners and dress codes, orderliness and timetables, and measures to preclude 'unhygienic' practices of various sorts. Paradoxically, such rules were perfectly compatible with the bourgeois ideal of independence, although ambiguity was evident too. Respect for the fine arts, for example, went hand in hand with a suspicion of Bohemian lifestyles [25: p. 9]. In other words, the compulsive bourgeois interest in following rules had an up-side and a down-side. As we saw in Chapter 2, the bourgeoisie believed that the rest of society should adhere to their codes of social conduct – at work and at play, within the family and outside it. But all too often this belief was transformed into strident insistence and moralising intemperance, both of which revealed pervasive feelings of bourgeois self-doubt.

A new historical consensus about the Wilhelmine bourgeoisie is apparent only in outline. A good example is the question that prompted debate even during Wilhelm's reign: how 'feudal' was imperial Germany [13; 127; Mosse in 140]? This question provided the kernel of the so-called 'feudalisation thesis', which some 'Bielefelders' now argue should be referred to as the 'aristocratisation thesis'. Many historians think neither thesis is convincing. In their view the bourgeoisie displayed such marked self-sufficiency and self-reliance that to talk of its being feudalised or aristocratised in any way is grossly misleading. These historians concede that a minority of industrial magnates may have sought titles from the state; many mimicked the lifestyle of Junkers by building ostentatious mansions; and many concluded marriage alliances among their 'betters'. But most upper-middle-class Germans displayed a conspicuous *lack* of interest in those avenues of social advancement that have been most emphasised by proponents of the feudalisation thesis. Instead they tended to arrange their social calendars to permit interaction with the same upper-middle-class colleagues with which they had everyday business dealings; this was especially true among Jewish businessmen. They also exhibited a remarkable determination to press their own class interests even when this necessitated conflict with the old nobility. In short: although most members of the German bourgeoisie feared revolution, respected the state, and opposed full democracy, this does not mean they took their cue from a 'feudal' élite [13; 25; 281].

The precariousness of consensus on this issue is interesting on two further counts. First, much of the evidence used on both sides can actually be read two ways. Second, Anglo-American scholars seem more eager to put the final nail in the coffin of the feudalisation thesis than do their German colleagues. On most other questions concerning the bourgeoisie, however, the jury is still out. How are we to push ahead with research on German liberalism, recognising that it was rooted in the bourgeoisie but not identifying it exclusively with a single class [intro. and Langewiesche in 117; Langewiesche in 141; Sheehan in 155; 256]? If either the German bourgeoisie or German liberalism is compared with other middle-class groups and movements in Europe, does the German path still appear unique [e.g. Mommsen and Eley in 155]? If we take 1914 as our benchmark instead of 1933, was bourgeois development leading toward long-term success or disaster [18: p. 230; 53: intro.; 152: pt iv, chs 7 and 8; 175: ch. 15; 177: chs 8 and 9; Chickering in 197]? The fact that such specific questions remain on the agenda bodes well for future scholarship.

The Lower Middle Classes

Like the bourgeoisie, the German *Mittelstand* or *Kleinbürgertum* can be subdivided, in this case into an 'old' and a 'new' *Mittelstand*. The old *Mittelstand* consisted mainly of such traditional groups as craftsmen, shopkeepers, small businessmen, and peasants. The new *Mittelstand* included white-collar workers, other salaried employees, low-ranking public officials, and shop clerks [91; Kocka in 112]. The old *Mittelstand* has been described as 'pre-industrial', and its outlook as 'anti-modern', because it was the group that profited least from Germany's rapid industrialisation. The new *Mittelstand*, by contrast, was created, sustained, and enlarged by industrialisation. Some historians believe that certain elements of the new *Mittelstand*, for example upper-level managers, are more appropriately included in the *Bürgertum*.

The *Mittelstand* has long attracted special attention because of its alleged susceptibility to fascism. It bears noting that historians have recently reassessed two previous assumptions about Nazism: that it was essentially an 'extremism of the centre', and that the lower-middle classes provided the Nazi Party with most of its voters. Nevertheless, this research has *not* overturned the hypothesis that the Nazis drew their most active members, leaders, and programmatic ideas from lower-middle-class sources. Therefore, the nature of *Mittelstand* discontents and petty-bourgeois activism remain compelling subjects even for German historians not directly concerned with Nazism. Indeed, many historians still consider the 1890s to have been decisive in the process whereby the old *Mittelstand* drifted from its revolutionary stance in 1848, failed to find a secure lodging on the right, and eventually succumbed to Hitler's promises of social prestige and economic prosperity. Volker Berghahn drew a picture of the *Mittelstand*'s essentially passive response to manipulation from above: 'here was a potential group of voters which responded to the emotional propaganda of the conservative elites and was waiting to be organised. And organised they became' [17: p. 162; see also Childers in 25].

To date only a handful of historians have contributed critiques of this view. Pulling these critiques together provides the outline of a four-point remedial programme [22: ch. 5; Haupt and Lenger in 155; Crossick in 278]. We need, first, a more concrete and differentiated consideration of such imprecise categories as shop-

101

keepers, craftsmen, and peasants. We must also consider how contemporaries understood and used these terms, and how their meanings changed over time. Second, the material divisions within each section of the *Mittelstand* must be appreciated: similar features of industrialisation threatened some elements of the *Mittelstand* and created new opportunities for others. Third, there was a great ambiguity to social relations between the *Mittelstand* and those classes above and below it. Until more studies are conducted on upward and downward mobility, intra-family exploitation, and generational conflicts, we will not fully understand the mixed forces of attraction and repulsion that contributed to the self-definition of the *Mittelstand*. Fourth and lastly, further investigation is needed into the linkages between *Mittelstand* politics and the broader development of mass politics after 1890. We still know very little about which elements of the Wilhelmine *Mittelstand* were susceptible to those 'modern' political devices – demagoguery, charisma, and physical intimidation – that played such a role in Hitler's rise to power.

Until recently, German peasants and rural workers were the two most forgotten components of rural society [Farr in 68; 201; Saul in 272; Flemming in 278; primary texts in 133: chs 8 and 9; 231: ch. 7]. Rural workers alone now deserve this designation, for studies of German peasants have proliferated of late [Jacobeit in 140: vol. 2; Moeller intro. in 172]. Some early sceptics published essays in the 1970s to reveal a peasantry that was not as prone to make 'irrational' economic decisions as historians once believed. But the revisionist assault assumed major proportions in the mid-1980s [22: ch. 6; 110; 171]. In this work there is a new appreciation for the complexity of cultural life in the German countryside. The alleged dichotomy between peasants and lords, for instance, is seen now to have been intersected by gender issues, family networks, village traditions, and estate economies [Catt, Hagen, Kaschuba, and Schulte in 68]. Studies of rural mentalities are also providing an important complement to previous work on the relationship between peasants and the SPD. What has emerged from this research is a picture of peasant protest that was much more voluble and volatile than scholars once believed. As a new brand of rural demagogue emerged, the complacency of traditional party practices – the politics of 'Ja' and 'Amen' – departed the countryside forever.

The Working Classes and Workers' Culture

Early studies of the Social Democratic Party sought to explore its triumphs and shortcomings by focusing on theoretical debates within the SPD, on prominent party leaders and intellectuals, and on the ways in which the state and big business reacted to the threat of revolution. Although much of this scholarship reflected the 'top-down' approach that prevailed in the 1960s and 1970s, it provided many crucial insights into the actual mechanisms whereby state authority and class interest combined to suppress working-class emancipation. This research has been sustained and redirected in recent years, but by no means has it been thrown overboard [221; Ritter intro. in 229; 230; 244; 278]. That the process of realignment has been gradual is demonstrated by the obvious connections between such older themes as the role of feminism within the labour movement and – not at all the same question – newer studies of women's place within the industrial workforce [61; 63: ch. 5; Daniel and Frevert in 79; 82; 83: chs 9, 12, and 13; 208].

Most historians now agree that it is incorrect to conceive of the German working classes as ascribing to positions that were either uniformly reformist or uniformly revolutionary [221: chs 2 and 3; 254]. Yet they still disagree about how workers perceived their own interests and responded to discrimination. One set of answers is provided by historians who study the labour movement. Scholars previously tended to consider the role of the SPD in isolation and overestimated the common worker's understanding of theoretical debates. Newer research, by contrast, stresses the diversity of German labour; it also analyses in a more sophisticated way how ideology was actually transmitted to workers and understood by them. Thus historians are examining strikes, lock-outs, and such individual forms of protest as alcoholism and absenteeism [229: sec. iv; 248; Geary in 278]. They are also distinguishing between the tendency of trade unions to concentrate on long-term achievements and individual workers' short-term concerns within life and labour cycles. As early views of a sharp disjunction between a revolutionary SPD leadership and a reformist rank-and-file are reconsidered, the reluctance of trade unions to commit themselves to strikes has necessitated greater attention to the grey area between economic and political protest [Geary in 67; 104; 193; Geary in 278; compare Geary and Eley in 79].

Another set of answers is provided by historians who study workers' culture [1; 63: chs 3 and 4; 182; 225; 228; 230: ch. 9; Lidtke in 278]. They do so in part because institutional studies of the SPD told us so little about the concrete experiences of individual workers in the workplace, in school, within the family and neighbourhood, and at leisure. To be sure, the best contributions to this genre overlap with more conventional political perspectives. There still exists a danger that if social history and political history diverge too far we may find ourselves trying to write the history of Germany's working classes with the SPD entirely left out [54: ch. 7]. That being said, historians of workers' culture charge that older interpretations conceived of German workers as 'passive receptacles waiting to be filled with ideas poured down from above', not as free actors making rational decisions about their best interests [60: chs 5 and 6, esp. p. 25; 160; 242]. The reaction to this viewpoint has fuelled a tremendous growth in the history of everyday life (*Alltagsgeschichte*). Although *Alltagsgeschichte* has recently been hailed as the 'most important new departure in West German historiography during the last decade', it has arguably made more impact on the study of the Third Reich than of Wilhelmine Germany [56: p. 297; 112: intro.; 224: pp. 34-7; 230: ch. 9]. Yet the necessary conceptual tools are now at hand.

Historians of the *Alltag* use a broad conception of 'culture' – the 'bricks and mortar' of our everyday experience – to explore the forces shaping far more than just working-class leisure activities. In this way we have gained a new window on workplace experiences, social mobility, communal environment, housing, health, family life, religion, education, reading habits, and those elements of popular culture discussed in Chapter 2 [1; intro., esp. pp. 40-3, and Brüggemeier and Niethammer in 112; 182; 248]. There is also a growing interest in the 'rough' side of working-class culture. To explain how workers deviated from bourgeois Germans in their social values and norms, we have already considered the issue of prostitution. Historians are also turning to working-class crime, heavy drinking, fairs and carnivals, and such common workplace practices as sabotage, pilferage, and horse-play. All this requires great diligence in locating appropriate sources and analysing them intelligently [e.g. 63: ch. 6]. Yet far from constituting a casual or trivial side of workers' culture, law-breaking and other patterns of non-conformity can help us assess the degree to which workers were integrated into society. In this way conventional distinctions between the 'public' and the 'private' are being rethought. Never before have historians had open to them more avenues to discover the inner experiences of life in the Wilhelmine age.

Which Germany?

The student of German society might be prompted at this point to ask *which* of the classes explored in this chapter actually set the tone of intellectual, cultural, and political life in the empire. This is exactly the issue historians have addressed with studies of Germany's 'dominant', 'hegemonic', and 'alternative' cultures. This prompts a second query. To what degree did members of *all* social classes feel they belonged to a single nation, a single society, or a single political culture?

In proposing one among many possible answers, let us consider where the scholarly debate about Wilhelmine Germany stood twenty years ago and where it stands now. Here it appears that something quite revolutionary has happened. In the midst of an increasing *plurality* of method, a *convergence* of views has occurred among historians. It has occurred, moreover, principally on analytical terrain that only a short time ago seemed no more fertile than any other: the history of the German bourgeoisie. How might we sketch the contours of this new (partial) consensus? It is always unfair to take the work of one or two scholars as representative of opinion within a broad international community of colleagues. There may none the less be some value in considering two leading figures in the debate, Hans-Ulrich Wehler and Thomas Nipperdey, and contrasting their accounts [for Wehler, 291; 292: ch. 20; 295; and Wehler in 139; for Nipperdey, 190: ch. 15; 191: ch. 10; 192: vol. 1, ch. 17; and 192: vol. 2, 'Schluß'].

Wehler and Nipperdey address the same central questions from opposite starting points. Wehler recently posed the question: how bourgeois was imperial Germany? Nipperdey has asked: was Wilhelmine society dominated by a subject mentality – was it an *Untertanen-Gesellschaft*? In both cases we might expect the answer to be in the affirmative. This is certainly how both begin. Wehler argues that Germany before 1914 was dynamic and capitalistic in a fully modern sense. It was pluralistic, protective of civil liberties, and reformist (especially in local government). It was even characterised by a public sphere that allowed great latitude to critics of authority. '*But*', Wehler concludes, despite its 'undeniable modernity', Wilhelmine society was also a society of subjects. Moreover, it was a society that first revealed the 'pathology' of the German bourgeoisie, leading to 1933. The discrediting of liberal politics, the appearance of a new brand of nationalism (*Reichsnationalismus*), and the undermining of neo-humanist ideals of *Bildung* left in place traditional and anachronistic obstructions that contributed to the 'fragility' of the bourgeoisie during the Weimar Republic. 'In this sense', concludes Wehler, '1933 was the payback [*Quittung*] for bourgeois conservatism and nationalism, for bourgeois hesitancy to risk a bid for power, for the deficits of liberal-bourgeois political culture' [139: pp. 276–7 and *passim*].

Nipperdey's trajectory is Wehler's inverse. Citing both the caricature and the reality in Heinrich Mann's *Man of Straw*, Nipperdey concedes that much about Wilhelmine society was indeed uncivil. Much about it was also unbourgeois. This was, as Max Weber argued, a society deeply imprinted by authoritarian and bureaucratic habits of mind. Wilhelmine nationalism was of a new sort: expansionist, anti-democratic, and 'perhaps' even pre-fascist. It suffered from many institutional blockages to reform, most obviously in Prussia. And like the Kaiser himself, Wilhelmine society was both 'protean' and 'hollow', pathetically theatrical and inwardly insecure [see also 22: ch. 3]. On this basis, Nipperdey, like Wehler, concedes that the 'lack of political-bourgeois culture' was one of Weimar's greatest burdens. '*But*', Nipperdey concludes, German society before 1914 was a society based on the rule of law, a society of relative 'liberality', of 'normalcy'. 'On the way to modern pluralism', it was capable of self-reform and of self-criticism. It had left behind the nineteenth century with few regrets. It was a society in crisis, perhaps. But it had already – 'from within' – embraced bourgeois and liberal values sufficiently to reveal 'the growing potential for a future democracy' [191: p. 185; 192: vol. 2, p. 880].

What are we to conclude from this? Clearly, sharp differences of opinion between Wehler and Nipperdey have given way to more modest ones of nuance and tone. Both historians have explicitly endorsed 'ambivalence on principle'. Both, unabashedly, have gravitated toward a 'yes, but . . .' position. This slipperiness is not welcomed in all quarters. For some observers it signifies a positive step forward, an attempt to avoid the trap of thinking in black and white terms; but for others it simply makes honest, straightforward debate more difficult [e.g. 66; Langewiesche in 117; Blackbourn in 139; Sheehan and Mommsen in 155]. Does it really matter, though, what comes *before* the all-important 'but' and what comes *after*? A qualified 'yes' is in order here – it does matter quite a bit. Yet the convergence of views is the more important point.

One might argue, furthermore, that Wehler and Nipperdey still appear to conflate the terms 'bourgeois' and 'liberal'. As distinct social and political categories, these terms are not magically reconciled in the world of 'political culture', as the cited passages tend to suggest. Lastly, these two historians still diverge on specific points: for example, the degree to which the military was impervious to bourgeois influence. This suggests that older positions have not been abandoned altogether. *But* – in the end it would be wrong to overemphasise these shortcomings and points of divergence. The many areas of interpretation where Wehler and Nipperdey agree are exactly those areas where the most intensive and convincing research has been conducted over the past two decades. 'In the totality [*das Ganze*] lies the truth', Nipperdey has written, 'and the totality requires patience' [192: vol. 1, p. 838]. As historians have tried to chart a viable path among the many Germanies revealed since 1960, patience – supplemented with diligence and insight – has paid a handsome reward.

Conclusions

The reader was warned at the outset to expect no grand synthesis, no unitary viewpoint, no happy ending to the search for German history's Holy Grail. It may provide cold comfort to know that experts gathered at a recent conference to discuss imperial Germany concluded that a 'master narrative' may no longer be attainable (if it ever was). The assembled scholars could only agree to disagree – on the very first day – about what research agendas might prevail in the future [57]. Why is this so? This book has tried to suggest four groups of answers. These can be recapitulated briefly under the following rubrics: (1) the role of present political and scholarly environments; (2) the pluralisation of interpretative models; (3) a new appreciation of diversity within the German empire itself; and (4) the open-endedness of all history.

1 Wilhelmine historiography has been highly contentious for at least thirty-five years. German historical writing has often been tempted onto the shoals of political debate about such current problems as access to decision-making, gender relations, equality of opportunity, national identity, multiculturalism, and the need to come to terms with Germany's recent past. In Germany, but not only there, scholarship has been pursued in changing political contexts. When Fritz Fischer demanded a new confrontation with Germany's past in 1961, he prompted a break with conservative thinking that had dominated the German historical guild since 1945. From that point on, the medium of German historical writing was inextricably linked with its message. When new forms of political pluralism and student protest renewed the assault on traditionalism in the late 1960s, the substance and tone of writing on Wilhelmine Germany changed again. Approaches favoured in the 1970s and 1980s are now being challenged by a more conservative, nationalist viewpoint. Yet there are signs that the pluralistic

liberal outlook will prevail in the immediate future, and these signs are welcome.

We can be less sanguine about the extent to which German and Anglo-American scholars actually read each others' books today compared to, say, twenty years ago. The sheer volume of published work is almost overwhelming. But that in itself does not explain what some observers perceive as a growing disinclination among scholars on both sides of the Atlantic to digest and debate the views of colleagues outside their national community. The preceding chapters have identified a number of issues where German and non-German scholars disagree. The different university systems in Germany, Britain, and North America cannot be excluded as factors here. That holders of coveted professorial chairs in Germany have criticised the history of everyday life for idealising and romanticising the masses emphasises the importance of understanding these institutional contexts. Because academic environments will continue to evolve under the impact of social and political challenges, views about how we should write history will not stand still either.

2 Any attempt to sum up the 'essential' features of life in Wilhelmine Germany is determined by our overall conceptual and methodological approach. Even when we seek to determine, as we have in this book, how Germans reacted to the idea of change itself, we can find in Wilhelmine Germany more or less what we go looking for. By now it should be apparent that not every German in the empire was equally 'moved' when a new colony in east Africa was founded, when a wildcat strike was suppressed, when a local zoo was established, when a Polish estate was confiscated, when a law of assembly was liberalised, when the price of bread fell by 5 Pfennigs, when the first woman entered a German university, or when Sergei Diaghilev's Ballets russes introduced avant-garde dance to the German stage. The different yardsticks, interpretative models, and research strategies we use to measure the most 'immediate' events of an age yield many different answers. We know that Diaghilev's company left a trail of 'excitement, incredulity, and rapture' when it toured Berlin shortly before the First World War [52a: p. 26]. But could not exactly the same emotions of excitement, incredulity, and rapture – or similarly *intense* ones – have been generated by the other historical events just catalogued,

109

depending on the perspective of the individual? This book has sought to prompt reflection on exactly this question.

To say this is not to suggest that we rebuild our image of the past from the ground up whenever a new interpretation is introduced. An emphasis on historical deconstruction and 'new directions' does not mean that we throw out older research because it was undertaken prior to the most recent interpretative turning point. A much more useful approach is to take what is valuable from past analyses, combine it with what we find convincing from newer work, and then identify the remaining questions that catch our imagination as historians. As James J. Sheehan has written, a phenomenon like liberalism needs less to be defined according to universal or normative yardsticks than investigated empirically with specific, descriptive measures [155: p. 29].

3   The diversity of Wilhelmine Germany forces the historian to apply an eclectic methodology to concrete historical problems. Two such problems have been highlighted in our analysis: the multiplicity of identities among the German people, and the regional diversity of life in the empire. These two problems are obviously related: identity is based on experience. Previous chapters have revealed not one Germany but many. Wilhelmine Germany was deeply divided by cleavages based upon geography, ethnicity, class, religion, and gender. Class continues to be the most common yardstick historians use to try to measure the social 'distance' between in-groups and out-groups. It is against this scale that we most often try to gauge whether German society was becoming polarised before 1914. Yet class-based analysis is most fruitful when supplemented with a methodology that pays attention to cultural factors. Wilhelm's subjects did not classify themselves in mutually exclusive categories. Rather, different categories of privilege and status intersected with one another to define identity. Thinking in these terms helps bring to life the everyday world of out-groups in a way that was formerly possible only for the study of great statesmen, who of course are more reliable in leaving a written record of their life. For example, it permits an unusual degree of empathy with one of the most striking figures of the Wilhelmine age, Rosa Luxemburg – a Pole, a socialist, a Jew, and a woman [186].

110

Local and regional identities, too, are coming more sharply into focus. This is partly the cause, partly the consequence, of new models and interpretations. When scholars in the 1960s wrote loosely about the 'Prusso-German empire' and neglected developments in Bavaria, Saxony, Baden, Württemberg, and the smaller states of the empire, they opened the door for another perspective. Historians have successfully resisted the temptation to discard the central question that Hans-Ulrich Wehler and John Röhl answered so differently – 'Who ruled in Berlin?' – with the narrow substitute, 'Who ruled in Munich?' (or Dresden, or Karlsruhe, or Stuttgart). Instead they have begun to address problems of political consciousness and the *interrelationship* of local, regional, and national identities. The peculiarities rather than the uniformity of circumstances in the different regions of Germany largely determined how the rise of mass politics was accommodated or incompletely deflected. They also decisively influenced class relationships, nationality conflicts, and religious controversies.

4   It now seems fair to conclude that whereas the *Sonderweg* concept once had heuristic value, its time has passed. Larger issues of continuity, on the other hand, remain as compelling and contentious as ever. The Nazi stain on German history and its relevance for a younger generation have not been wiped away by political and scholarly reorientations in the 1980s, despite attempts to achieve exactly this aim. Those searching for something closer to the ideal of a modern, pluralistic, tolerant, and democratic society continue to look to the Wilhelmine era for evidence that German history in the twentieth century might have turned out other than it did. This book has not advocated that students engage in the kind of counter-factual 'what if' history that invariably proves untenable. It has none the less tried to convey a sense of the openness of all history by suggesting that from the perspective of 1918 the calamities that befell Germany, Europe, and the world between 1933 and 1945 were anything but inevitable.

This account began with Thomas Nipperdey's trumpet-call to attention: in the beginning was Bismarck. It is appropriate that it ends with Nipperdey too, signalling his unparalleled achievement in describing the imperial age. Nipperdey concluded that German history before 1918 is not simply 'the' pre-history of 1933. It was

111

none the less 'a' history that *did* lead to 1933, as it might have led to other outcomes. It is, continues Nipperdey, not simply a history of 'failure and collapse'. Nor is it one of 'success and glory'. 'It is both, and both hang together: greatness and danger' [192: vol. 1, p. 813; 192: vol. 2, p. 877]. To understand this history – this *ensemble* of histories – one perspective will not do. Structures of domination, understandings of work, varieties of experience, meanings of language: all these aspects of Wilhelmine life require different historical approaches. Social groups and social conflicts cannot be examined only 'from above'. Economic development did not follow nineteenth-century patterns exclusively. Political systems need illumination as processes. Foreign policy cannot be divorced from domestic influences. Gender relations were subject to strategies for hegemony. The Great War opened certain paths to the future and closed off others.

Students can be understandably impatient with the 'yes, but . . .' mode of analysis. In trying to balance actual and interpretative diversities fairly, the judiciousness that makes this approach so even-handed can become bland and uninspiring. In fact an alternative lies at hand. As Richard J. Evans has observed, it is not necessarily correct to suggest that the basic tone of good historical analysis is always grey – neither black nor white but perceptible in infinite shades [66: p. 137]. History is *not* grey. It is bursting with colour. This book has tried to convey an appreciation for the rich hues of history: those that actually existed in the past and those available for analysis today. From that palette the student of Wilhelmine Germany can paint any number of new portraits.

Select Bibliography

The following selection of works on Wilhelmine Germany is weighted heavily toward English-language readers, especially students and non-specialists. In some cases an English essay has been included in place of a German monograph (sometimes by the same author). In other cases a work is included because it offers an up-to-date guide to further literature, a broad range of viewpoints, or a particularly innovative approach. Although contributors to edited collections could not be cited individually here, many of these are identified in the text references.

Items that might constitute core readings for a teaching unit on Wilhelmine Germany have been marked with a single asterisk. Items that include especially useful primary materials – including contemporary texts, statistics, and illustrations – are marked with a double asterisk.

[1]   *Lynn Abrams, *Workers' Culture in Imperial Germany: Leisure and Recreation in the Rhineland and Westphalia* (London, New York, 1992).

[2]   *Lynn Abrams, *Bismarck and the German Empire, 1871–1918* (London, New York, 1995).

[3]   Lynn Abrams, 'Prostitutes in Imperial Germany, 1870–1918: Working Girls or Social Outcasts?', in Richard J. Evans (ed.), *The German Underworld* (London, 1988) pp. 189–209.

[4]   Lynn Abrams, 'From Control to Commercialization. The Triumph of Mass Entertainment in Germany, 1900–1925', *German History*, vol. 8, no. 3 (1990) pp. 278–93.

[5]   Lynn Abrams, 'Martyrs or Matriarchs? Working-class Women's Experience of Marriage in Germany before the First World War', *Women's History Review*, vol. 1 (1992) pp. 357–76.

[6]   James C. Albisetti, *Secondary School Reform in Imperial Germany* (Princeton, NJ, 1983).

[7]   James C. Albisetti, *Schooling German Girls and Women: Secondary and Higher Education in the Nineteenth Century* (Princeton, NJ, 1988).

[8]   *Ann Taylor Allen, *Satire and Society in Wilhelmine Germany: Kladderadatsch & Simplicissimus 1890–1914* (Lexington, Ky., 1984).

[9] Ann Taylor Allen, *Feminism and Motherhood in Germany, 1800–1914* (New Brunswick, NJ, 1991).

[10] Margaret Lavinia Anderson, 'Voter, Junker, *Landrat*, Priest: the Old Authorities and the New Franchise in Imperial Germany', *American Historical Review*, vol. 98 (1993) pp. 1448–74.

[11] Celia Applegate, *A Nation of Provincials: The German Idea of Heimat* (Berkeley, Calif., 1990).

[12] Robert B. Armeson, *Total Warfare and Compulsory Labor: A Study of the Military-Industrial Complex in Germany During World War I* (The Hague, 1964).

[13] Delores L. Augustine, *Patricians & Parvenus: Wealth and High Society in Wilhelmine Germany* (Oxford, Providence, RI, 1994).

[14] Klaus J. Bade (ed.), *Population, Labour and Migration in 19th- and 20th-century Germany* (Leamington Spa, Hamburg, New York, 1987).

[15] Kenneth D. Barkin, *The Controversy over German Industrialization, 1890–1902* (Chicago, 1970).

[16] Volker R. Berghahn, *Der Tirpitz-Plan. Genesis und Verfall einer innenpolitischen Krisenstrategie unter Wilhelm II.* (Düsseldorf, 1971).

[17] *Volker R. Berghahn, *Germany and the Approach of War in 1914*, 2nd edn (London, 1993; originally published 1973).

[18] *Volker R. Berghahn, *Imperial Germany 1871–1914: Economy, Society, Culture and Politics* (Providence, RI, Oxford, 1994).

[19] **Volker R. Berghahn and Wilhelm Deist (eds), *Rüstung im Zeichen der wilhelminischen Weltpolitik: Grundlegende Dokumente 1890–1914* (Düsseldorf, 1988).

[20] Richard Bessel, *Germany after the First World War* (Oxford, 1993).

[21] David Blackbourn, *Class, Religion and Local Politics in Wilhelmine Germany: The Centre Party in Württemberg before 1914* (New Haven, Conn., 1980).

[22] *David Blackbourn, *Populists and Patricians: Essays in Modern German History* (London, 1987).

[23] David Blackbourn, 'New Legislatures: Germany, 1871–1914', *Historical Research*, vol. 65 (1992) pp. 201–14.

[24] *David Blackbourn and Geoff Eley, *The Peculiarities of German History: Bourgeois Society and Politics in Nineteenth-Century Germany* (Oxford, 1984; originally published 1980).

[25] *David Blackbourn and Richard J. Evans (eds), *The German Bourgeoisie* (London, 1991).

[26] Richard Blanke, *Prussian Poland in the German Empire (1871–1900)* (New York, 1981).

[27] Olaf Blaschke and Frank-Michael Kuhlemann (eds), *Religion und Milieu im deutschen Kaiserreich* (Gütersloh, in press, 1995).

[28] Werner K. Blessing, 'The Cult of Monarchy, Political Loyalty and the Workers' Movement in Imperial Germany', *Journal of Contemporary History*, vol. 13 (1978) pp. 357–75.

[29] Gary Bonham, *Ideology and Interests in the German State* (New York, 1991).

[30] Knut Borchardt, *Perspectives on Modern German Economic History and Policy*, trans. Peter Lambert (Cambridge, 1991).

[31] Karl Erich Born, *Wirtschafts- und Sozialgeschichte des Deutschen Kaiserreichs (1867/71–1914)* (Stuttgart, 1985).

114

[32] Warren G. Breckman, 'Disciplining Consumption: The Debate about Luxury in Wilhelmine Germany, 1890–1914', *Journal of Social History*, vol. 24 (1991) pp. 485–505.

[33] Thomas M. Bredohl, 'Parishioners, Priests and Politicians: The Centre Party in the Rhineland, 1890–1914', Ph.D. dissertation, University of Toronto (1995).

[34] Gerhard Bry, *Wages in Germany 1871–1945* (Princeton, NJ, 1960).

[35] *Central European History*, vol. 18 (1985), 'Symposium: The Censorship of Literary Naturalism'.

[36] *Central European History*, vol. 22 (1989), special issue, 'German Histories: Challenges in Theory, Practice, Technique'.

[37] Gerald Chapple and Hans H. Schulte (eds), *The Turn of the Century: German Literature and Art, 1890–1915* (Bonn, 1981).

[38] Roger Chickering, *Imperial Germany and a World Without War: The Peace Movement and German Society, 1892–1914* (Princeton, NJ, 1975).

[39] *Roger Chickering, We Men Who Feel Most German: A Cultural Study of the Pan-German League, 1886–1914* (Boston, Mass., 1984)

[40] Roger Chickering, *Karl Lamprecht: A German Academic Life (1856–1915)* (Atlantic Highlands, NJ, 1993).

[41] Roger Chickering, 'Casting their Gaze More Broadly: Women's Patriotic Activism in Imperial Germany', *Past & Present*, no. 118 (1988) pp. 156–85.

[42] Roger Chickering, 'Patriotic Societies and German Foreign Policy, 1890–1914', *International History Review*, vol. 1 (1979) pp. 470–89.

[43] Werner Conze and Jürgen Kocka (eds), *Bildungsbürgertum im 19. Jahrhundert*, pt 1 (Stuttgart, 1985).

[44] **W. A. Coupe, *German Political Satires from the Reformation to the Second World War*, pt II, *1849–1918*, 2 vols (White Plains, NY, 1987).

[45] David F. Crew, *Town in the Ruhr: A Social History of Bochum, 1860–1914* (New York, 1979).

[46] Ashok V. Desai, *Real Wages in Germany 1871–1913* (Oxford, 1968).

[47] Marion F. Deshmukh, 'German Impressionist Painters and World War I', *Art History*, vol. 4/1 (1981) pp. 66–79.

[48] Raymond Dominick, 'Nascent Environmental Protection in the Second Empire', *German Studies Review*, vol. 9 (1986) pp. 257–91.

[49] Andreas Dorpalen, *German History in Marxist Perspective* (Detroit, Mich., 1988).

[50] Jost Dülffer and Karl Holl (eds), *Bereit zum Krieg. Kriegsmentalität im wilhelminischen Deutschland 1890–1914* (Göttingen, 1986).

[51] *Jack R. Dukes and Joachim Remak (eds), *Another Germany: A Reconsideration of the Imperial Era* (Boulder, Colo., 1988).

[52] Christiane Eisenberg, 'Fußball in Deutschland 1890–1914. Ein Gesellschaftsspiel für bürgerliche Mittelschichten', *Geschichte und Gesellschaft*, vol. 20 (1994) pp. 181–210.

[52a] Modris Eksteins, *Rites of Spring: The Great War and the Birth of the Modern Age* (Toronto, 1989).

[53] Geoff Eley, *Reshaping the German Right: Radical Nationalism and Political Change after Bismarck*, 2nd edn (Ann Arbor, Mich., 1991; originally published 1980).

115

[54]   *Geoff Eley, *From Unification to Nazism: Reinterpreting the German Past* (Boston, Mass., 1986).

[55]   Geoff Eley, 'The View from the Throne: the Personal Rule of Kaiser Wilhelm II', *Historical Journal*, vol. 28 (1985) pp. 469–85.

[56]   Geoff Eley, 'Labor History, Social History, *Alltagsgeschichte*: Experience, Culture, and the Politics of the Everyday – A New Direction for German Social History?', *Journal of Modern History*, vol. 61 (1989) pp. 297–343.

[57]   *Geoff Eley (ed.), *Society, Culture, and the State in Germany, 1870–1930* (Ann Arbor, Mich., 1995, in press).

[58]   Michael Epkenhans, *Die wilhelminische Flottenrüstung, 1908–1914* (Munich, 1991).

[59]   Richard J. Evans, *The Feminist Movement in Germany, 1894–1933* (London, 1976).

[60]   *Richard J. Evans, *Rethinking German History: Nineteenth-Century Germany and the Origins of the Third Reich* (London, Boston, 1987).

[61]   Richard J. Evans, *Comrades and Sisters: Feminism, Socialism and Pacifism in Europe, 1870–1945* (Brighton, 1987).

[62]   Richard J. Evans, *Death in Hamburg: Society and Politics in the Cholera Years, 1830–1910* (Oxford, 1987).

[63]   Richard J. Evans, *Proletarians and Politics: Socialism, Protest and the Working Class in Germany before the First World War* (New York, 1990).

[64]   Richard J. Evans, 'Prostitution, State and Society in Imperial Germany', *Past & Present*, no. 70 (1976) pp. 106–29.

[65]   Richard J. Evans, 'Upstairs, Downstairs in the Central European Home', *Archiv für Sozialgeschichte*, vol. 27 (1987) pp. 628–40.

[66]   Richard J. Evans, 'Nipperdeys Neunzehntes Jahrhundert. Eine kritische Auseinandersetzung', *Geschichte und Gesellschaft*, vol. 20 (1994) pp. 119–39.

[67]   *Richard J. Evans (ed.), *Society and Politics in Wilhelmine Germany* (London, 1978).

[68]   Richard J. Evans and W.R. Lee (eds), *The German Peasantry* (New York, 1986).

[69]   Brett Fairbairn, *Election Battles: German Politics, the Parties, and the Reichstag Campaigns of 1898–1903* (1996, in press).

[70]   Brett Fairbairn, 'Authority vs. Democracy: Prussian Officials and the German Elections of 1898–1903', *Historical Journal*, vol. 33 (1990) pp. 811–38.

[71]   Gerald D. Feldman, *Army, Industry and Labor in Germany, 1914–1918* (Providence, RI, 1992; originally published 1966).

[72]   **Hans Fenske (ed.), *Unter Wilhelm II. 1890–1918* (Darmstadt, 1982).

[73]   **Hans Fenske (ed.), *Quellen zur deutschen Innenpolitik 1890–1914* (Darmstadt, 1991).

[74]   Niall Ferguson, 'Germany and the Origins of the First World War: New Perspectives', *Historical Journal*, vol. 35 (1992) pp. 725–52.

[75]   Niall Ferguson, 'Public Finance and National Security: The Domestic Origins of the First World War Revisited', *Past & Present*, no. 142 (1994) pp. 141–68.

[76]   Fritz Fischer, *Germany's Aims in the First World War* (London, 1967; originally published 1961).

116

[77]   Fritz Fischer, *War of Illusions: German Policies 1911-1914* (New York, 1975; originally published 1969).

[78]   *Fritz Fischer, *From Kaiserreich to Third Reich: Elements of Continuity in German History 1871-1945*, trans. Roger Fletcher (London, 1986; originally published 1979).

[79]   Roger Fletcher (ed.), *Bernstein to Brandt: A Short History of German Social Democracy* (London, 1987).

[80]   John C. Fout, 'Sexual Politics in Wilhelmine Germany: The Male Gender Crisis, Moral Purity, and Homophobia', *Journal of the History of Sexuality*, vol. 2 (1992) pp. 388-421.

[81]   *John C. Fout (ed.), *German Women in the Nineteenth Century: A Social History* (New York, London, 1984).

[82]   Barbara Franzoi, *At the Very Least She Pays the Rent: Women and German Industrialization, 1871-1914* (Westport, Conn., 1985).

[83]   *Ute Frevert, *Women in German History: From Bourgeois Emancipation to Sexual Liberation* (Oxford, Hamburg, New York, 1988; originally published 1986).

[84]   Ute Frevert (ed.), *Bürgerinnen und Bürger. Geschlechterverhältnisse im 19. Jahrhundert* (Göttingen, 1988).

[85]   Dieter Fricke *et al.* (eds), *Lexikon zur Parteiengeschichte. Die bürgerlichen und kleinbürgerlichen Parteien und Verbände in Deutschland (1789-1945)*, 4 vols (Leipzig, 1983-6).

[86]   Ronald A. Fullerton, 'Toward a Commercial Popular Culture in Germany: the Development of Pamphlet Fiction 1871-1914', *Journal of Social History*, vol. 12 (1979) pp. 489-511.

[87]   Lothar Gall and Dieter Langewiesche (eds), *Liberalismus und Region. Zur Geschichte des deutschen Liberalismus im 19. Jahrhundert* (Munich, 1995).

[88]   Peter Gay, *Freud, Jews and Other Germans. Masters and Victims in Modernist Culture* (New York, 1978).

[89]   **Imanuel Geiss, *July 1914: The Outbreak of the First World War – Selected Documents*, trans. H. M. Hughes and I. Geiss (London, 1967; originally published 1963-4).

[90]   *Imanuel Geiss, *German Foreign Policy, 1871-1914* (London, 1976).

[91]   Robert Gellately, *The Politics of Economic Despair: Shopkeepers and German Politics 1890-1914* (London, Beverly Hills, Calif., 1974).

[92]   Michael Geyer, 'The Stigma of Violence, Nationalism, and War in Twentieth-Century Germany', *German Studies Review*, special issue, 'German Identity' (Winter 1992) pp. 75-110.

[93]   Dieter Groh, *Negative Integration und revolutionärer Attentismus. Die deutsche Sozialdemokratie am Vorabend des Ersten Weltkrieges* (Frankfurt a.M., 1973).

[94]   William W. Hagen, *Germans, Poles, and Jews: The Nationality Conflict in the Prussian East, 1772-1914* (Chicago, 1970).

[95]   Alex Hall, *Scandal, Sensation, and Social Democracy: The SPD Press and Wilhelmine Germany, 1890-1914* (Cambridge, 1977).

[96]   Beverly Heckart, *From Bassermann to Bebel: The Grand Bloc's Quest for Reform in the Kaiserreich* (New Haven, Conn., 1974).

[97]   Linda A. Heilman, 'Industrial Unemployment in Germany: 1873-1913', *Archiv für Sozialgeschichte*, vol. 27 (1987) pp. 25-49.

117

[98]   Karl Helfferich, *Germany's Economic Progress and National Wealth, 1888–1913* (Berlin, 1913).

[99]   Volker Hentschel, *Wirtschaft und Wirtschaftspolitik im wilhelminischen Deutschland* (Stuttgart, 1978).

[100] Holger H. Herwig, *The German Naval Officer Corps: A Social and Political History, 1890–1918* (Oxford, 1973).

[101] Holger H. Herwig, *'Luxury' Fleet: The Imperial German Navy, 1888–1918* (London, Boston, Mass., 1980).

[102] Holger H. Herwig, *Hammer or Anvil? Modern Germany 1648–Present* (Lexington, Mass., Toronto, 1994).

[103] *Holger H. Herwig (ed.), *The Outbreak of World War I: Causes and Responsibilities*, 5th rev. edn (Lexington, Mass., Toronto, 1991).

[104] Stephen Hickey, *Workers in Imperial Germany: The Miners of the Ruhr* (Oxford, 1985).

[105] Klaus Hildebrand, *Deutsche Aussenpolitik 1871–1918* (Munich, 1989).

[106] **Walther G. Hoffmann *et al.*, *Das Wachstum der deutschen Wirtschaft seit der Mitte des 19. Jahrhunderts* (Berlin, 1965).

[107] **Gerd Hohorst, Jürgen Kocka, and Gerhard A. Ritter (eds), *Sozialgeschichtliches Arbeitsbuch II. Materialien zur Statistik des Kaiserreichs 1870–1914*, 2nd edn (Munich, 1978).

[108] Isabel V. Hull, *The Entourage of Kaiser Wilhelm II, 1888–1918* (New York, Cambridge, 1982).

[109] James C. Hunt, *The People's Party in Württemberg and Southern Germany 1890–1914* (Stuttgart, 1975).

[110] James C. Hunt, 'The "Egalitarianism" of the Right: the Agrarian League in Southwest Germany, 1893–1914', *Journal of Contemporary History*, vol. 10 (1975) pp. 513–30.

[111] Gangolf Hübinger and Wolfgang J. Mommsen (eds), *Intellektuelle im Deutschen Kaiserreich* (Frankfurt a.M., 1993).

[112] *Georg Iggers (ed.), *The Social History of Politics: Critical Perspectives in West German Historical Writing since 1945* (Leamington Spa, 1985).

[113] Konrad H. Jarausch, *The Enigmatic Chancellor: Bethmann Hollweg and the Hubris of Imperial Germany* (New Haven, Conn., 1973).

[114] Konrad H. Jarausch, *Students, Society, and Politics in Imperial Germany* (Princeton, NJ, 1982).

[115] Konrad H. Jarausch, 'The Illusion of Limited War: Chancellor Bethmann Hollweg's Calculated Risk, July 1914', *Central European History*, vol. 2 (1969) pp. 48–76.

[116] Konrad H. Jarausch, 'Revising German History: Bethmann Hollweg Revisited', *Central European History*, vol. 21 (1988) pp. 224–43.

[117] Konrad H. Jarausch and Larry Eugene Jones (eds), *In Search of a Liberal Germany: Studies in the History of German Liberalism from 1789 to the Present* (New York, Oxford, 1990).

[118] Peter Jelavich, *Munich and Theatrical Modernism: Politics, Playwriting, and Performance 1890–1914* (Cambridge, Mass., 1985).

[119] Peter Jelavich, *Berlin Cabaret* (Cambridge, Mass., 1993).

[120] Hartmut John, *Das Reserveoffizierkorps im Deutschen Kaiserreich 1890–1914* (Frankfurt a.M., New York, 1981).

[121] Michael John, *Politics and the Law in Late Nineteenth-Century Germany: The Origins of the Civil Code* (Oxford, 1989).

[122] Michael John, *The German Empire 1867–1914: Problems of Interpretation* (London, 1996, in press).

[123] Eric A. Johnson, 'The Roots of Crime in Imperial Germany', *Central European History*, vol. 15 (1982) pp. 351–76.

[124] Jeffrey A. Johnson, *The Kaiser's Chemists: Science and Modernization in Imperial Germany* (Chapel Hill, NC, 1990).

[125] *Larry Eugene Jones and James Retallack (eds), *Elections, Mass Politics, and Social Change in Modern Germany: New Perspectives* (Cambridge, New York, 1992).

[126] Larry Eugene Jones and James Retallack (eds), *Between Reform, Reaction, and Resistance: Studies in the History of German Conservatism from 1789 to 1945* (Providence, RI, Oxford, 1993).

[127] Hartmut Kaelble, 'Wie feudal waren die deutschen Unternehmer im Kaiserreich? Ein Zwischenbericht', in Richard Tilly (ed.), *Beiträge zur quantitativen vergleichenden Unternehmensgeschichte* (Stuttgart, 1985) pp. 148–71.

[128] *David E. Kaiser, 'Germany and the Origins of the First World War', *Journal of Modern History*, vol. 55 (1983) pp. 442–74.

[129] Marion A. Kaplan, *The Jewish Feminist Movement in Germany: The Campaigns of the Jüdischer Frauenbund 1904–1938* (Westport, Conn., 1979).

[130] *Marion A. Kaplan, *The Making of the Jewish Middle Class: Women, Family, and Identity in Imperial Germany* (Oxford, 1991).

[131] Marion A. Kaplan, 'Prostitution, Morality Crusades, and Feminism', *Women's Studies International Forum*, vol. 5 (1982) pp. 619–27.

[132] Eckart Kehr, *Economic Interest, Militarism, and Foreign Policy*, ed. Gordon A. Craig, trans. Grete Heinz (Berkeley, Calif., 1977).

[133] **Alfred Kelly (ed. and trans.), *The German Worker: Working-Class Autobiographies from the Age of Industrialization* (Berkeley and Los Angeles, Calif., 1987).

[134] Katherine D. Kennedy, 'Regionalism and Nationalism in South German History Lessons, 1871–1914', *German Studies Review*, vol. 12 (1989) pp. 11–33.

[135] Martin Kitchen, *The German Officer Corps, 1890–1914* (Oxford, 1968).

[136] Martin Kitchen, *The Silent Dictatorship: The Politics of the German High Command under Hindenburg and Ludendorff, 1916–1918* (London, 1976).

[137] Jürgen Kocka, *Facing Total War: German Society, 1914–18*, trans. Barbara Weinberger (Leamington Spa, 1984; originally published 1973).

[138] *Jürgen Kocka, 'German History before Hitler: The Debate about the German Sonderweg', *Journal of Contemporary History*, vol. 23 (1988) pp. 3–16.

[139] Jürgen Kocka (ed.), *Bürger und Bürgerlichkeit im 19. Jahrhundert* (Göttingen, 1987).

[140] Jürgen Kocka (ed.) with Ute Frevert, *Bürgertum im 19. Jahrhundert. Deutschland im europäischen Vergleich*, 3 vols (Munich, 1988).

[141] *Jürgen Kocka and Allan Mitchell (eds), *Bourgeois Society in Nineteenth-Century Europe* (Oxford, Providence, RI, 1993).

119

[142] Thomas A. Kohut, *Wilhelm II and the Germans: A Study in Leadership* (Oxford, New York, 1991).

[143] Marven H. Krug, 'Civil Liberties in Imperial Germany', Ph.D. dissertation, University of Toronto (1995).

[144] John J. Kulczycki, *School Strikes in Prussian Poland, 1901-1907: The Struggle over Bilingual Education* (New York, 1981)

[145] John J. Kulczycki, *The Foreign Worker and the German Labor Movement: Xenophobia and Solidarity in the Coal Fields of the Ruhr, 1871-1914* (Oxford, Providence, RI, 1994).

[146] Thomas Kühne, *Dreiklassenwahlrecht und Wahlkultur in Preussen, 1867-1914* (Düsseldorf, 1994).

[147] Brian Ladd, *Urban Planning and Civic Order in Germany, 1860-1914* (Cambridge, Mass., 1990).

[148] Simone Lässig, Karl Heinrich Pohl, and James Retallack (eds), *Modernisierung und Region. Studien zu Wahlen, Wahlrecht und Politischer Kultur im Wilhelminischen Deutschland* (Bielefeld, 1995, in press).

[149] Marjorie Lamberti, *Jewish Activism in Imperial Germany: The Struggle for Civil Equality* (New Haven, Conn., 1978).

[150] Marjorie Lamberti, *State, Society, and the Elementary School in Imperial Germany* (Oxford, New York, 1989).

[151] *John W. Langdon, *July 1914: The Long Debate, 1918-1990* (New York, Oxford, 1991).

[152] Dieter Langewiesche, *Liberalismus in Deutschland* (Frankfurt a.M., 1988).

[153] Dieter Langewiesche, 'Das Deutsche Kaiserreich – Bemerkungen zur Diskussion über Parlamentarisierung und Demokratisierung Deutschlands', *Archiv für Sozialgeschichte*, vol. 19 (1979) pp. 628-42.

[154] Dieter Langewiesche (ed.), *Ploetz. Das deutsche Kaiserreich 1867/71 bis 1918* (Freiburg, Würzburg, 1984).

[155] Dieter Langewiesche (ed.), *Liberalismus im 19. Jahrhundert. Deutschland im europäischen Vergleich* (Göttingen, 1988).

[156] Andrew Lees, 'Debates about the Big City in Germany, 1890-1914', *Societas*, vol. 5 (1975) pp. 31-48.

[157] Robin Lenman, 'Art, Society and the Law in Wilhelmine Germany: the Lex Heinze', *Oxford German Studies*, vol. 8 (1973) pp. 86-113.

[158] Katherine Anne Lerman, *The Chancellor as Courtier: Bernhard von Bülow and the Governance of Germany, 1900-1909* (Cambridge, 1990).

[159] Richard S. Levy, *The Downfall of the Anti-Semitic Political Parties in Imperial Germany* (New Haven, Conn., 1975).

[160] *Vernon Lidtke, *The Alternative Culture: Socialist Labor in Imperial Germany* (New York, Oxford, 1985).

[161] Vernon Lidtke, 'Social Class and Secularisation in Imperial Germany. The Working Classes', *Leo Baeck Institute Yearbook*, vol. 25 (1980) pp. 21-40.

[162] Derek S. Linton, 'Who has the Youth has the Future': The Campaign to Save Young Workers in Imperial Germany* (Cambridge, 1991).

[163] Wilfried Loth, *Katholiken im Kaiserreich. Der politische Katholizismus in der Krise des wilhelminischen Deutschlands* (Düsseldorf, 1984).

[164] Wilfried Loth (ed.), *Deutscher Katholizismus im Umbruch zur Moderne* (Stuttgart, 1991).

[165]   Heinrich Mann, *Man of Straw* (originally published in German as *Der Untertan*) (Harmondsworth, Middx., 1984).

[166]   Kevin McAleer, *Dueling: The Cult of Honor in Fin-de-Siècle Germany* (Princeton, NJ, 1994).

[167]   Charles E. McClelland, *State, Society and University in Germany, 1700-1914* (Cambridge, 1980).

[168]   Akiba Mendel, 'The Debate between Prussian Junkerdom and the Forces of Urban Industry 1897-1902', *Jahrbuch des Instituts für Deutsche Geschichte*, vol. 4 (1975) pp. 301-38.

[169]   Sibylle Meyer, 'The Tiresome Work of Conspicuous Leisure: On the Domestic Duties of the Wives of Civil Servants in the German Empire (1871-1918)', in Marilyn J. Boxer and Jean H. Quataert (eds), *Connecting Spheres* (New York, 1987) pp. 156-65.

[170]   Robert G. Moeller, 'Dimensions of Social Conflict in the Great War: The View from the German Countryside', *Central European History*, vol. 14 (1981) pp. 142-68.

[171]   Robert G. Moeller, 'Peasants and Tariffs in the Kaiserreich: How Backward Were the *Bauern*?', *Agricultural History*, vol. 55 (1981) pp. 370-84.

[172]   Robert G. Moeller, 'The Kaiserreich Recast? Continuity and Change in Modern German Historiography', *Journal of Social History*, vol. 17 (1984) pp. 655-83.

[173]   Robert G. Moeller (ed.), *Peasants and Lords in Modern Germany: Recent Studies in Agricultural History* (Boston, Mass., 1986).

[174]   Wolfgang J. Mommsen, *Max Weber and German Politics, 1890-1920*, trans. Michael S. Steinberg (Chicago, 1980; originally published 1959).

[175]   *Wolfgang J. Mommsen, *Der autoritäre Nationalstaat. Verfassung, Gesellschaft und Kultur im deutschen Kaiserreich* (Frankfurt a.M., 1990) (forthcoming in trans. as *Imperial Germany 1867-1918: Politics, Culture, and Society in an Authoritarian State* (London, 1995).

[176]   Wolfgang J. Mommsen, *Grossmachtstellung und Weltpolitik 1870-1914. Die Außenpolitik des Deutschen Reiches* (Frankfurt a.M., Berlin, 1993).

[177]   Wolfgang J. Mommsen, *Bürgerliche Kultur und künstlerische Avantgarde 1870-1918* (Frankfurt a.M., Berlin, 1994).

[178]   Wolfgang J. Mommsen, *Bürgerstolz und Weltmachtstreben, 1890 bis 1918* (Frankfurt a.M., Berlin, 1995, in press).

[179]   Wolfgang J. Mommsen, 'Public Opinion and Foreign Policy in Wilhelmian Germany, 1897-1914', *Central European History*, vol. 24 (1991) pp. 381-401.

[180]   Wolfgang J. Mommsen, 'Kaiser Wilhelm II and German Politics', *Journal of Contemporary History*, vol. 25 (1990) pp. 289-316.

[181]   Werner E. Mosse and Arnold Paucker (eds), *Juden im wilhelminischen Deutschland 1890-1914* (Tübingen, 1976).

[182]   Dietrich Mühlberg (ed.), *Proletariat: Culture and Lifestyle in the 19th Century* (Leipzig, 1988).

[183]   Lysbeth W. Muncy, *The Junker in the Prussian Administration under William II, 1888-1914* (Providence, RI, 1944).

[184]   Richard C. Murphy, *Guestworkers in the German Reich: A Polish Community in Wilhelmian Germany* (New York, 1983).

[185]   Sebastian Müller, 'Official Support and Bourgeois Opposition in Wil-

121

helminian Culture', in Irit Rogoff (ed.), *The Divided Heritage* (Cambridge, 1991) pp. 163–90.

[186]   J. P. Nettl, *Rosa Luxemburg*, abridged edn (New York, 1989; originally published in 2 vols, 1966).

[187]   *New German Critique*, vol. 29 (1983), special issue, 'Mass Culture'.

[188]   J. Alden Nichols, *Germany after Bismarck: The Caprivi Era, 1890–1894* (Cambridge, Mass., 1958).

[189]   Thomas Nipperdey, *Die Organisation der deutschen Parteien vor 1918* (Düsseldorf, 1961).

[190]   Thomas Nipperdey, *Gesellschaft, Kultur, Theorie. Gesammelte Aufsätze zur neueren Geschichte* (Göttingen, 1976).

[191]   Thomas Nipperdey, *Nachdenken über die deutsche Geschichte* (Munich, 1986).

[192]   Thomas Nipperdey, *Deutsche Geschichte 1866–1918*, 2 vols: vol. 1, *Arbeitswelt und Bürgergeist*, 2nd edn (Munich, 1991); vol. 2, *Machtstaat vor der Demokratie* (Munich, 1992).

[193]   Mary Nolan, *Social Democracy and Society: Working-Class Radicalism in Düsseldorf, 1890–1920* (Cambridge, New York, 1981).

[194]   Christoph Nonn, *Verbraucherprotest und Parteiensystem im wilhelminischen Deutschland* (Düsseldorf, 1995, in press).

[195]   James M. Olson, 'Nationalistic Values in Prussian Schoolbooks prior to World War I', *Canadian Review of Studies in Nationalism*, vol. 1 (1973) pp. 47–59.

[196]   Thomas J. Orsagh, 'The Probable Geographical Distribution of German Income, 1882–1962', *Zeitschrift für die gesamte Staatswissenschaft*, vol. 124 (1968) pp. 280–311.

[197]   Walter Pape (ed.), *1870/71–1989/90: German Unifications and the Change of Literary Discourse* (Berlin, 1993).

[198]   *Peter Paret, *The Berlin Secession: Modernism and its Enemies in Imperial Germany* (Cambridge, Mass., 1980).

[199]   Peter Paret, 'The Artist as "Staatsbürger": Aspects of the Fine Arts and the Prussian State Before and During the First World War', *German Studies Review*, vol. 6 (1983) pp. 421–37.

[200]   Peter Paret and Beth Irwin Lewis, 'Art, Society, and Politics in Wilhelmine Germany', *Journal of Modern History*, vol. 57 (1985) pp. 696–710.

[201]   J. A. Perkins, 'The German Agricultural Worker 1815–1914', *Journal of Peasant Studies*, vol. 11 (1984) pp. 3–27.

[202]   Hartmut Pogge von Strandmann and R. J. W. Evans (eds), *The Coming of the First World War*, 2nd edn (Oxford, 1990; originally published 1988).

[203]   Karl Heinrich Pohl, 'Obrigkeitsstaat und Demokratie. Aspekte der "Revolution" von 1918/19', in Manfred Hettling (ed.), *Revolution in Deutschland? 1789–1989* (Göttingen, 1991) pp. 46–69.

[204]   */**Ian Porter and Ian D. Armour, *Imperial Germany 1890–1918* (London, 1991).

[205]   Hans-Jürgen Puhle, *Agrarische Interessenpolitik und preußischer Konservatismus im wilhelminischen Reich 1893–1914* (Bonn, 1975; originally published 1966).

[206]   *Peter G. J. Pulzer, *The Rise of Political Anti-Semitism in Germany and Austria*, 2nd edn (London, 1988; originally published 1964).

[207]   *Peter G. J. Pulzer, *Jews and the German State: The Political History of a Minority, 1848–1933* (Oxford, 1992).

[208]   *Jean H. Quataert, *Reluctant Feminists in German Social Democracy, 1885–1917* (Princeton, NJ, 1979).

[209]   Joachim Radkau, 'Die wilhelminischen Ära als nervöses Zeitalter, oder: Die Nerven als Netz zwischen Tempo- und Körpergeschichte', *Geschichte und Gesellschaft*, vol. 20 (1994) pp. 211–41.

[210]   Manfred Rauh, *Föderalismus und Parlamentarismus im Wilhelminischen Reich* (Düsseldorf, 1973).

[211]   Manfred Rauh, *Die Parlamentarisierung des Deutschen Reiches* (Düsseldorf, 1977).

[212]   Nancy R. Reagin, '"A True Woman Can Take Care of Herself": The Debate over Prostitution in Hanover, 1906', *Central European History*, vol. 24 (1991) pp. 347–80.

[213]   Herbert Reinke, '"Armed as if for a War": The State, the Military and the Professionalisation of the Prussian Police in Imperial Germany', in Clive Emsley and Barbara Weinberger (eds), *Policing Western Europe* (New York, 1991) pp. 55–73.

[214]   James Retallack, *Notables of the Right: The Conservative Party and Political Mobilization in Germany, 1876–1918* (London, Boston, Mass., 1988).

[215]   *James Retallack, 'Social History with a Vengeance? Some Reactions to H.-U. Wehler's "Das Deutsche Kaiserreich"', *German Studies Review*, vol. 7 (1984) pp. 423–50.

[216]   James Retallack, 'Anti-Semitism, Conservative Propaganda, and Regional Politics in Late Nineteenth-Century Germany', *German Studies Review*, vol. 11 (1988) pp. 377–403.

[217]   James Retallack, '"What is to Be Done?" The Red Specter, Franchise Questions, and the Crisis of Conservative Hegemony in Saxony, 1896–1909', *Central European History*, vol. 23 (1990) pp. 271–312.

[218]   James Retallack, 'From Pariah to Professional? The Journalist in German Society and Politics, from the Late Enlightenment to the Rise of Hitler', *German Studies Review*, vol. 16 (1993) pp. 175–223.

[219]   James Retallack, 'Election Campaigns and Franchise Struggles in Regional Perspective', *German History*, vol. 13 (1995) pp. 70–79.

[220]   Gerhard Ritter, 'The Historical Foundations of the Rise of National-Socialism', in International Council for Philosophy and Humanistic Studies and UNESCO (eds), *The Third Reich* (London, 1955) pp. 381–416.

[221]   Gerhard A. Ritter, *Arbeiterbewegung, Parteien und Parlamentarismus* (Göttingen, 1976).

[222]   **Gerhard A. Ritter (with Merith Niehuss), *Wahlgeschichtliches Arbeitsbuch. Materialien zur Statistik des Kaiserreichs 1871–1918* (Munich, 1980).

[223]   Gerhard A. Ritter, *Die deutschen Parteien 1830–1914* (Göttingen, 1985).

[224]   *Gerhard A. Ritter, *The New Social History in the Federal Republic of Germany* (London, 1991).

[225]   Gerhard A. Ritter, 'Workers' Culture in Imperial Germany: Problems and Points of Departure for Future Research', *Journal of Contemporary History*, vol. 13 (1978) pp. 165–90.

[226] Gerhard A. Ritter (ed.), *Gesellschaft, Parlament und Regierung. Zur Geschichte des Parlamentarismus in Deutschland* (Düsseldorf, 1974).

[227] **Gerhard A. Ritter (ed.), *Das Deutsche Kaiserreich 1871–1914. Ein historisches Lesebuch*, 2nd edn (Göttingen, 1975; originally published 1967).

[228] Gerhard A. Ritter (ed.), *Arbeiterkultur* (Königstein, 1979).

[229] Gerhard A. Ritter (ed.) (with Elisabeth Müller-Luckner), *Der Aufstieg der deutschen Arbeiterbewegung* (Munich, 1990).

[230] *Gerhard A. Ritter and Klaus Tenfelde, *Arbeiter im Deutschen Kaiserreich 1871 bis 1914* (Bonn, 1992).

[231] **Gerhard A. Ritter and Jürgen Kocka (eds), *Deutsche Sozialgeschichte 1870–1914. Dokumente und Skizzen*, 3rd edn (Munich, 1982).

[232] Stuart T. Robson, 'Left-Liberalism in Germany, 1900–1919', D.Phil. thesis, University of Oxford (1966).

[233] John C.G. Röhl, *Germany Without Bismarck: The Crisis of Government in the Second Reich, 1890–1900* (London, 1967).

[234] John C.G. Röhl, *The Kaiser and his Court: Wilhelm II and the Government of Germany*, trans. Terence F. Cole (Cambridge, 1994; originally published 1987).

[235] *John C.G. Röhl and Nicolaus Sombart (eds), *Kaiser Wilhelm II: New Interpretations* (Cambridge, 1982).

[236] Karl Rohe, *Wahlen und Wählertraditionen in Deutschland* (Frankfurt a.M., 1992).

[237] *Karl Rohe (ed.), *Elections, Parties and Political Traditions: Social Foundations of German Parties and Party Systems, 1867–1987* (New York, Oxford, Munich, 1990).

[238] Thomas Rohkrämer, *Der Militarismus der 'kleinen Leute'. Die Kriegervereine im Deutschen Kaiserreich 1871–1914* (Munich, 1990).

[239] John D. Rolling, 'Liberals, Socialists and City Government in Imperial Germany: the Case of Frankfurt am Main, 1900–1918', Ph.D. dissertation, University of Wisconsin – Madison (1979).

[240] Arthur Rosenberg, *Imperial Germany: The Birth of the German Republic 1871–1918*, trans. Ian Morrow (Boston, Mass., 1967; originally published 1931).

[241] *Ronald J. Ross, *Beleaguered Tower: The Dilemma of Political Catholicism in Wilhelmine Germany* (Notre Dame, Ind., 1976).

[242] Guenther Roth, *The Social Democrats in Imperial Germany: A Study in Working-Class Isolation and Negative Integration* (Totowa, NJ, 1963).

[243] Reinhard Rürup, *Emanzipation und Antisemitismus. Studien zur 'Judenfrage' der bürgerlichen Gesellschaft* (Frankfurt a.M., 1987; originally published 1975).

[244] Klaus Saul, *Staat, Industrie, Arbeiterbewegung im Kaiserreich* (Düsseldorf, 1974).

[245] Klaus Saul, 'Der "Deutsche Kriegerbund". Zur innenpolitischen Funktion eines "nationalen" Verbandes im kaiserlichen Deutschland', *Militärgeschichtliche Mitteilungen*, no. 1 (1969) pp. 95–169.

[246] Klaus Saul, 'Der Kampf um die Jugend zwischen Volksschule und Kaserne. Ein Beitrag zur "Jugendpflege" im Wilhelminischen Reich 1890–1914', *Militärgeschichtliche Mitteilungen*, no. 1 (1971) pp. 97–143.

[247] Klaus Saul, 'Der Staat und die "Mächte des Umsturzes." Ein Beitrag zu den Methoden antisozialistischer Repression und Agitation vom Scheitern des Sozialistengesetzes bis zur Jahrhundertwende', *Archiv für Sozialgeschichte*, vol. 12 (1972) pp. 293–350.

[248] **Klaus Saul *et al.* (eds), *Arbeiterfamilien im Kaiserreich. Materialien zur Sozialgeschichte in Deutschland 1871–1914* (Düsseldorf, 1982).

[249] Wolfgang Schieder and Volker Sellin (eds), *Sozialgeschichte in Deutschland*, 4 vols (Göttingen, 1986–7).

[250] **Jürgen Schmädcke, *Wählerbewegung im wilhelminischen Deutschland*, 2 vols (Berlin, 1994).

[251] Gustav Schmidt, 'Innenpolitische Blockbildungen in Deutschland am Vorabend des Ersten Weltkrieges', *Aus Politik und Zeitgeschichte*. Beilage zur Wochenzeitung 'Das Parlament' (13 May 1972) pp. 3–32.

[252] David Schoenbaum, *Zabern 1913: Consensus Politics in Imperial Germany* (London, 1982).

[253] *Gregor Schöllgen (ed.), *Escape into War? The Foreign Policy of Imperial Germany* (Oxford, New York, Munich, 1990).

[254] *Carl Schorske, *German Social Democracy, 1905–1917: The Development of the Great Schism* (Cambridge, Mass., 1983; originally published 1955).

[255] Wolfgang Schwentker, 'Die alte und die neue Aristokratie. Zum Problem von Adel und bürgerliche Elite in den deutschen Sozialwissenschaften 1900–30', in École Francaise de Rome (ed.), *Les noblesses européennes au XIXe siècle* (Rome, 1988) pp. 659–84.

[256] *James J. Sheehan, *German Liberalism in the Nineteenth Century* (Chicago, 1978).

[257] James J. Sheehan, 'Liberalism and the City in Nineteenth-Century Germany', *Past & Present*, no. 51 (1971) pp. 116–37.

[258] *James J. Sheehan (ed.), *Imperial Germany* (New York, London, 1976).

[259] Dennis E. Showalter, 'German Grand Strategy: A Contradiction in Terms?', *Militärgeschichtliche Mitteilungen*, vol. 48, no. 2 (1990) pp. 65–102.

[260] Dennis E. Showalter, 'The Political Soldiers of Bismarck's Germany: Myths and Realities', *German Studies Review*, vol. 17 (1994) pp. 59–77.

[261] Helmut Walser Smith, *German Nationalism and Religious Conflict: Culture, Ideology, Politics, 1870–1914* (Princeton, NJ, 1995).

[262] Nicolaus Sombart, *Die deutschen Männer und ihre Feinde* (Munich, 1991).

[263] Elaine Glovka Spencer, *Police and the Social Order in German Cities: The Düsseldorf District, 1848–1914* (DeKalb, Ill., 1992).

[264] Reinhard Spree, *Health and Social Class in Imperial Germany*, trans. S. McKinnon-Evans (Oxford, New York, 1988).

[265] Nicholas Stargardt, *The German Idea of Militarism: Radical and Socialist Critics, 1866–1914* (New York, Cambridge, 1994).

[266] Gary D. Stark, *Entrepreneurs of Ideology: Neoconservative Publishers in Germany, 1890–1933* (Chapel Hill, NC, 1981).

[267] Gary D. Stark, 'Pornography, Society, and the Law in Imperial Germany', *Central European History*, vol. 14 (1981) pp. 200–29.

[268] Gary D. Stark, 'Cinema, Society, and the State: Policing the Film Industry in Imperial Germany', in Gary D. Stark and Bede K. Lackner (eds), *Essays*

on *Culture and Society in Modern Germany* (College Station, Tx., 1982) pp. 122–66.

[269]   Gary D. Stark, 'Trials and Tribulations: Authors' Responses to Censorship in Imperial Germany, 1885–1914', *German Studies Review*, vol. 12 (1989) pp. 447–68.

[270]   James D. Steakley, *The Homosexual Emancipation Movement in Germany* (New York, 1975).

[271]   Dirk Stegmann, *Die Erben Bismarcks. Parteien und Verbände in der Spätphase des Wilhelminischen Deutschlands* (Cologne, 1970).

[272]   Dirk Stegmann, Bernd-Jürgen Wendt, and Peter-Christian Witt (eds), *Deutscher Konservatismus im 19. und 20. Jahrhundert* (Bonn, 1983).

[273]   George Steinmetz, *Regulating the Social: The Welfare State and Local Politics in Imperial Germany* (Princeton, NJ, 1993).

[274]   Fritz Stern, *The Politics of Cultural Despair: A Study in the Rise of the Germanic Ideology* (Berkeley and Los Angeles, Calif., 1974; originally published 1961).

[275]   Michael Stürmer, *Das ruhelose Reich. Deutschland 1866–1918* (Berlin, 1983).

[276]   Michael Stürmer (ed.), *Das kaiserliche Deutschland. Politik und Gesellschaft 1870–1918* (Düsseldorf, 1984; originally published 1970).

[276a] Stanley Suval, *Electoral Politics in Wilhelmine Germany* (Chapel Hill, NC, 1985).

[277]   Uriel Tal, *Christians and Jews in Germany: Religion, Politics and Ideology in the Second Reich, 1870–1914* (Ithaca, NY, London, 1975).

[278]   *Klaus Tenfelde (ed.), *Arbeiter und Arbeiterbewegung im Vergleich* (= *Historische Zeitschrift*, Sonderheft 15) (Munich, 1986).

[279]   Klaus Theweleit, *Male Fantasies*, 2 vols (Minneapolis, 1987–9; originally published 1977–8).

[280]   Alastair Thompson, *The Strange Survival of German Liberalism: Left Liberals, the State, and Popular Politics in Wilhelmine Germany* (Oxford, 1995, in press).

[281]   Alastair Thompson, 'Honours Uneven: Decorations, the State and Bourgeois Society in Imperial Germany', *Past & Present*, no. 144 (1994) pp. 171–204.

[282]   Frank B. Tipton, *Regional Variations in the Economic Development of Germany during the Nineteenth Century* (Middletown, Conn., 1976).

[283]   Eleanor L. Turk, 'The Political Press and the People's Rights: The Role of the Political Press in the Debates over the Association Right in Germany, 1894–1899', Ph.D. dissertation, University of Wisconsin (1975).

[284]   Eleanor L. Turk, 'The Berlin Socialist Trials of 1896: An Examination of Civil Liberty in Wilhelmian Germany', *Central European History*, vol. 19 (1986) pp. 323–42.

[285]   Jeffrey T. Verhey, 'The "Spirit of 1914": The Myth of Enthusiasm and the Rhetoric of Unity in World War I Germany', Ph.D. dissertation, University of California, Berkeley (1991).

[286]   Shulamit Volkov, *Jüdisches Leben und Antisemitismus im 19. und 20. Jahrhundert* (Munich, 1990).

[287]   Klaus Vondung (ed.), *Das wilhelminische Bildungsbürgertum* (Göttingen, 1976).

[288]   Richard Wall and Jay Winter (eds), *The Upheaval of War: Family, Work and Welfare in Europe, 1914–1918* (Cambridge, 1988).

[289]   Donald G. Warren, Jr, *The Red Kingdom of Saxony: Lobbying Grounds for Gustav Stresemann, 1901–1909* (The Hague, 1964).
[290]   Steven B. Webb, 'Agricultural Protection in Wilhelminian Germany: Forging an Empire with Pork and Rye', *Journal of Economic History*, vol. 62 (1982) pp. 309–26.
[291]   *Hans-Ulrich Wehler, *The German Empire 1871–1918* (Leamington Spa, 1985; originally published 1973).
[292]   Hans Ulrich Wehler, *Krisenherde des Kaiserreichs 1871–1918*, 2nd rev. edn (Göttingen, 1979; originally published 1970).
[293]   *Hans-Ulrich Wehler, *Bibliographie zur neueren deutschen Sozialgeschichte* (Munich, 1993).
[294]   Hans-Ulrich Wehler, *Deutsche Gesellschaftsgeschichte*, vol. 3, *1849–1914. Von der 'Deutschen Doppelrevolution' bis zum Beginn des Ersten Weltkrieges* (Munich, 1995, in press).
[295]   Hans-Ulrich Wehler, 'Historiography in Germany Today', in Jürgen Habermas (ed.), *Observations on 'The Spiritual Situation of the Age'* (Cambridge, Mass., 1984) pp. 221–59.
[296]   Hans-Ulrich Wehler, 'What is the "History of Society"?', *Storia della storiografia*, vol. 18 (1990) pp. 5–19.
[297]   David A. Welch, 'Cinema and Society in Imperial Germany, 1905–1918', *German History*, vol. 8 (1990) pp. 28–45.
[298]   Dan S. White, *The Splintered Party: National Liberalism in Hessen and the Reich, 1867–1918* (Cambridge, Mass., 1976).
[299]   Peter Winzen, 'Prince Bülow's Weltmachtpolitik', *Australian Journal of Politics and History*, vol. 22 (1976) pp. 227–42.
[300]   Hans-Günter Zmarzlik, 'Das Kaiserreich in neuer Sicht?', *Historische Zeitschrift*, vol. 222 (1976) pp. 105–26.

Index

camps, political, 49–50
capitalism, 11, 20, 24, 27, 60, 75, 85, 94, 96
Caprivi, Leo von, 39, 78
Catholics, Catholicism, 45, 47, 55, 57–8, 60, 98; *see also* Centre Party, German; religion
censorship, 39, 60, 64, 70–1
Central Association of German Industrialists, 46
Centre Party, German, 45, 46, 47, 49, 58, 85
Chickering, Roger, 51
church, *see* religion
cinema, 68
cities, 5, 16, 26, 28, 29–33, 45, 65, 68, 91, 104
Civil Code, 62
civil liberties, 14, 34–5, 40–2, 44, 106; *see also* public sphere
class, 5, 27, 32, 33, 45–6, 58, 83, 88, 92, 95, 110; *see also* élites; social conflict; social mobility; social stratification
Claß, Heinrich, 51
cleavages, social, 5, 49, 57, 83, 91, 110; *see also* social conflict; social stratification
Colonial Society, 47
Conservative Party, German, 42–4, 82, 85
conservatives, conservatism, 36, 57, 60, 64, 94, 96, 101, 106
constitution, 10, 20, 34–9, 86, 90
Council of People's Commissars, 87
countryside, 6, 17, 26, 28, 29–32, 37, 48, 55, 57, 91, 102
coup d'état, 40–2
court, royal, 11, 92, 94
Criminal Code, 41
culture, 31–4, 39, 60, 64–72, 99
    as analytical category, 14, 50, 52, 53–4, 62, 67–8, 69–70, 72, 104, 110, 112
    popular, 67–9

Dahrendorf, Ralf, 67
Danes, 59

Delbrück, Hans, 40
democracy, democratisation, 4, 8, 11, 34, 37, 38, 54, 85, 86, 95, 96, 100, 106; *see also* parliament, parliamentarisation; Reichstag; *Sonderweg*
Diaghilev, Sergei, 109
Döblin, Alfred, 83
domestic truce, 83, 85
Dresden, 33, 67, 111
duelling, 63, 76, 77
Düsseldorf, 47

Ebert, Friedrich, 87
economy, 16–24, 75, 79, 84, 87, 89, 96
education, 22, 27, 32, 36, 54–7, 58, 62, 65, 68, 71, 76, 104, 106
Effi Briest, 94
Einstein, Albert, 65
Eisner, Kurt, 86
elections, electoral politics, 11, 17, 34, 36, 37, 42, 43, 45, 47–52, 62, 81, 83, 85; *see also* mass politics; parties, political
Eley, Geoff, 14, 51, 77, 96, 98
élites, 3, 8, 10, 11, 12, 14, 28, 35, 41, 51, 55, 92, 94–7, 101; see also bourgeoisie; nobility
ethnicity, ethnic relations, *see* Jews; minorities; Poles
Evans, Richard J., 14, 112

Fairbairn, Brett, 48
family, 5, 17, 53, 61, 62, 71, 89–90, 99, 102, 104
Fatherland Party, German, 86
Federal Council, 36–37
federalism, federal states, *see* regionalism, political aspects
feminism, *see* women; gender
Ferdinand, Franz, 10, 80
'feudalisation thesis', 55, 63, 76, 97, 99–100
First World War, 3, 8, 10, 46, 52, 57, 67, 83–91, 112
Fischer, Fritz, 9–10, 73, 80, 82, 86, 108
Fontane, Theodore, 94

129

foreign policy, 4, 9–10, 11, 12, 37, 44, 73–80, 112; *see also* 'primacy of domestic/foreign policy' question; *Weltpolitik*
Foucault, Michel, 70, 71
Fout, John, 63–64
France, 3, 11, 31, 45, 53, 57, 77–85 *passim*, 96, 99
Frevert, Ute, 63

Gall, Lothar, 74
Gay, Peter, 61
Geiss, Imanuel, 11
gender, 5, 14, 28, 61–4, 71–2, 89, 102, 112; *see also* sexuality; women
German Empire 1871-1918, The, 11, 12, 13, 34, 53
German Nationalism and Religious Conflict, 58
Germany's Aims in the First World War, 9
Gerschenkron, Alexander, 95
Geyer, Michael, 77
Göhre, Paul, 31
Groener, Wilhelm, 87
Groh, Dieter, 11
Guelphs, 59

Habermas, Jürgen, 70
Hamburg, 90
Hansa League, 46
Hauptmann, Gerhard, 66
Hausen, Karin, 61
health and hygiene, 22, 26, 32, 36, 64, 65, 72, 86, 89, 99, 104
Helfferich, Karl, 84
Hertling, Georg von, 85
Hessen, 47
Hildebrand, Klaus, 74
Hillgruber, Andreas, 74
Hindenburg Program, 84
Hindenburg, Paul von, 84, 85, 87
historical interpretations, differing, 2–7, 8–15, 20–1, 24–8, 32–3, 34–5, 37–42, 44–54 *passim*, 57, 58, 61–62, 64, 67, 68, 73, 79, 80, 84, 85, 88, 96, 97, 101, 103–4, 105–7, 108–12

Anglo-American and German, 38, 73, 100, 109
East German, 13, 15, 27, 40, 47, 68, 74, 75
open questions, 7, 15, 33, 42, 44–52 *passim*, 59, 64, 69, 77, 78, 81–3, 86, 87, 92, 93, 101–2, 105–7
Hitler, Adolf, 8, 9, 52, 86, 101, 102
Hohenlohe-Schillingsfürst, Chlodwig zu, 39
Holland, 87
Hugenberg, Alfred, 22
Hull, Isabel, 94

If I Were Kaiser, 51
Imperial- and Free Conservative Party, 42–4
Imperial League against Social Democracy, 47
imperialism, *see Weltpolitik*; foreign policy
Independent Social Democratic Party, 85, 87
industrialisation, 16–29, 44, 61, 98, 101, 102, 112
industry, industrialists, 3, 11, 28, 46, 49, 50, 58, 85, 88, 98, 103
interest groups, economic and nationalist, 10, 20, 34, 35, 44, 46, 47, 51, 52, 77
Italy, 78

Jarausch, Konrad, 57, 81
Jelavich, Peter, 33
Jews, Judaism, 2, 32, 51, 57, 59–61, 72, 98, 100; *see also* anti-Semitism
Joll, James, 75
July crisis, 1914, 2, 5, 6, 9–10, 12, 73–5, 77, 78, 80–3
Junkers, 27, 42, 44, 71, 76, 85, 94–6, 100; *see also* agrarians, agrarianism; nobility
Jutland, Battle of, 84

Kaase, Max, 35
Kaiser, *see* Wilhelm II
Kaplan, Marion, 61
Karlsruhe, 111

130